MW00652160

"This is an excellent point-by-[...] Hank Hanegraaff's preterist int[...] its ungrounded and unbiblica[...] method of interpretation that, [...] Scripture, would undermine the historic Christian faith."

> Dr. Norman L. Geisler
> Co-founder and long-time Dean
> Southern Evangelical Seminary
> Charlotte, NC

"In this refreshingly clear treatment of the premillennial position, Mark Hitchcock and Thomas Ice have done the Christian church a great service. They have provided a fair and historical evaluation of this biblical doctrine helping us see clearly its development and significance. In the face of unfounded attacks, these men provide a balanced hermeneutic that honors the integrity of Scripture. I was challenged, strengthened, and edified reading this book and, what's more, it kindled a new excitement in the soon return of our great Christ!"

> Skip Heitzig
> Senior Pastor
> Calvary Chapel Albuquerque, NM

"The impact of the book *The Apocalypse Code* has been far-reaching and disturbing to many Bible-believing people who have had a keen interest in Bible prophecy and end-time events. Dr. Mark Hitchcock and Dr. Thomas Ice have rendered a most valuable assistance to those who are looking for an answer to the book's preterist position. The attitude and statements of the book regarding the nation of Israel and its part in God's prophetic plans for the future are indeed disturbing and one wonders whether the author has truly understood the 2,566 references to Israel in the Bible! God has not rejected His people Israel or cancelled His "everlasting covenant" to them! The apostle Paul has made it abundantly clear in the book of Romans that a "partial blindness" is upon Israel that will one day be removed! May God use this book to open the eyes of God's people to the truths of the Bible, and to expose the fallacies and arguments of *The Apocalypse Code*!"

> Dr. David Hocking
> Radio Bible Teacher
> *Hope For Today* Radio Broadcast

"Is Revelation prophecy—or just history? Hank Hanegraaff challenged those who see the future in the book of Revelation. Now Mark Hitchcock and Thomas Ice deliver a thorough, readable response. If you want solid, dependable answers on how to interpret the book of Revelation, this is the book you need to read!"

Dr. Charles Dyer
Provost and Dean of Education
Moody Bible Institute
Chicago, IL

"Hank Hanegraaff's irresponsible statements concerning futurism and his own novel approach to eschatology have needed proper response. We can all be grateful that Drs. Ice and Hitchcock, who have long studied and interacted with the interpretive system adopted by Mr. Hanegraaff, have arisen to meet this challenge. To those who seek to understand what 'The Bible Answer Man' is—and is not saying—and what hope the prophetic Scriptures can truly give, this book really does have the answer!"

Randall Price, Ph.D.
Professor of Jewish Studies
School of Religion
Liberty University
Lynchburg, VA

"Hitchcock and Ice nail the coffin shut on the contemporary attempt to resurrect preterism from the eschatological morgue where it has been for the past 100 years. Don't miss their insightful study, biblical exegesis, and historical survey. *Breaking the Apocalypse Code* will stretch your mind, stir your soul and bless your heart."

Dr. Ed Hindson
Assistant Chancellor
Liberty University
Lynchburg, VA

# BREAKING
## THE APOCALYPSE
# CODE

SETTING THE RECORD STRAIGHT ABOUT THE END TIMES

## MARK HITCHCOCK
## THOMAS ICE

WITH FOREWORD BY CHUCK SMITH

THE WORD
FOR TODAY

P.O. Box 8000, Costa Mesa, CA 92628 • Web Site: www.twft.com • E-mail: info@twft.com

Breaking the Apocalypse Code
By Mark Hitchcock and Thomas Ice
Foreword by Chuck Smith

© 2007 The Word For Today
Published by The Word For Today
P.O. Box 8000, Costa Mesa, CA 92628
(800) 272-WORD (9673)
Web Site: www.twft.com
Email: info@twft.com

ISBN: 978-1-597-51-035-6

This book is dedicated to Pastor Chuck Smith of Calvary Chapel, Costa Mesa, CA for his sixty-year ministry of faithfully teaching God's Word, verse-by-verse. God has used his ministry to positively impact millions to love, learn, share, and obey Scripture. We especially appreciate Pastor Chuck's love and clear exposition of Bible prophecy and thank God for his ministry.

> "I have fought the good fight, I have finished the course, I have kept the faith; in the future there is laid up for me the crown of righteousness, which the Lord, the righteous Judge, will award to me on that day; and not only to me, but also to all who have loved His appearing."
>
> —2 Timothy 4:7–8

# table of contents

# BREAKING THE APOCALYPSE CODE

In Proverbs we learn that "as iron sharpens iron, so a man sharpens the countenance of his friend" (27:17). Today many interpretations of the Bible exist. Some are solid and built on a strong foundation; other interpretations are set in sand and tend to sink with further insight and study.

When different interpretations are found concerning a single issue, it is good to find clear thinkers to discuss and work through the various aspects of what the Bible has to say concerning the issue, coming to solid biblical conclusions regarding the subject at hand. When we do this we are, in a sense, enacting the Scripture of iron sharpening iron.

One such issue open for interpretation is the book of Revelation. There seem to be three major schools of thought, with several branches found in each: amillennialism, postmillennialism (with preterits), and premillennialism (with classic premillennialism). Each of these views has devoted followers, advocates, and scholars; however, reasonably speaking, not all three interpretations can be correct. There are too many variances for them to be so!

What is a person trying to understand the book of Revelation to do? Who is he to believe? What school of thought is he to follow? My advice to the person asking this question is to believe the clearest, most biblical teaching found on the subject, coming to conclusions based upon good biblical exegesis (study and interpretation) rooted in a reasoned understanding of the text.

Over the course of my sixty years as pastor and Bible teacher, I have had to deal with many controversial subjects. Instead of steering clear of them, I have chosen to study the text more carefully, seeking insight and understanding from the entire Bible. Once I felt the Bible was teaching a particular subject clearly and unabashedly, I too taught the subject with confidence, knowing that the weight of Scripture backed the position I was taking.

Hence, my strong pre-millennial teaching! I found early on in my ministry that the whole Bible did indeed teach this position, focusing in on the nation of Israel, the rapture of the church, the great tribulation, and Christ's second coming. I believe that the Bible clearly teaches that these events will transpire at the end of the age.

In the pages you are about to read, you will find a dialogue of "iron sharpening iron"— two men engaged in a cordial response to a book that has been released called *The Apocalypse Code.* Not only will you find Mr. Hitchcock's and Mr. Ice's research insightful, you will find their understanding of the Scripture engaging and their mode of biblical interpretation clear and reasoned. I invite you to read these pages with an open Bible and an open mind, and be inspired to discover the rich truths they espouse about the Lord's soon return.

*—Pastor Chuck Smith*

# PREFACE

Hank Hanegraaff's book *The Apocalypse Code* boldly claims on the front cover to tell us "what the Bible really says about the end times." But does it really deliver? Does Hanegraaff's new hermeneutical method he calls "e squared" and its application really square with the Bible? That is the question we seek to answer. That is what this book is about—exposing the cracks in *The Apocalypse Code*.

It is challenging to write a response toward or critique of another book, especially one that is as strident as *The Apocalypse Code*. But we believe that it is necessary to set the record straight concerning the proper eschatological method and model. We have both received numerous calls, emails, and questions from people who are confused and frustrated by Hanegraaff's book and radio broadcasts attacking dispensationalism and the *Left Behind* theology. We pray that this book can be used by the Lord to clear up some of the confusion and firmly establish our focus on the blessed hope.

In a fiction book he co-authored, titled *The Last Disciple*, Hanegraaff makes this irenic statement:

**The point here is not to call into question the orthodoxy of the *Left Behind* authors. We are committed to the same**

goals: reading the Bible for all its worth and inspiring the hope of the second coming of Christ. Collegial debate in the interest of truth, however, is essential to the health of the church, while we adhere to the Christian maxim: "In essentials, unity; in nonessentials, liberty; in all things, charity." We must debate the issue, but we need to divide over it. The point is to demonstrate the dangers inherent in the interpretive method they and other dispensationalists employ. (395)

Hanegraaff's often repeated maxim on his radio program is that eschatology is an intramural issue we can "debate but not divide over." However, the tone of *The Apocalypse Code* hardly displays a charitable, non-divisive tone. To the contrary, Hanegraaff's tone is frequently disparaging and demeaning, and in a few places verges on downright sub-Christian standards. The book borders on being a diatribe against dispensationalism in general and Tim LaHaye and the *Left Behind* series in particular. Following are some of his more inflammatory, divisive references to the futurist, dispensational viewpoint:

Hanegraaff refers to premillennialism of the early nineteenth century as "the religious obscurantism of 'the socially disinherited, psychologically disturbed, and theologically naïve'" (44).

He calls it "the evangelical death march toward the endgame of Armageddon" (48) and that dispensationalists are "bent on ensuring that the horrors of Armageddon become a self-fulfilling prophecy" (47).

He says concerning the dispensational view of Ezekiel 40–48, "the implications of this theology are as bizarre as they are blasphemous" (63). He repeats the same charge on pages 64 and 269n86. He uses the word "blasphemous" in several places in the book to describe various dispensational interpretations (63, 64). Concerning the dispensational view of unfulfilled prophecy relating to Israel, he says that it "borders on blasphemy" (225). He even plays the race card by calling LaHaye and dispensationalists who simply support the modern state of Israel "racists" (xx–xxiii).

He calls dispensationalism a "pseudoeschatology" and compares it to the "pseudoscience of eugenics" (69). Hanegraaff draws a lengthy, inexplicable parallel between the evolutionary theory of Charles Darwin and the dispensational teachings of J. N. Darby, both of which occurred in the early 1830s. He contends that just as Darwin's theory led to the nightmare of Hitler, Darby's teaching leads to "the nightmarish ending" of Armageddon. This comparison is unjustifiable. The only justifiable parallel one can draw between these two men is that they lived at the same time. Darwin's theories were the direct cause of the Nazi atrocities that followed his views, but how can Darby's teachings cause the events of the tribulation that will be produced by God Himself? It is difficult to understand why Hanegraaff recklessly chose to make these comparisons rather than simply presenting his view and then defending it.

Here are a few of the condescending statements he makes toward those who disagree with his view:

- "Certainly no one is so *benighted* as to think . . . " (84, italics added).

- "Those today who *narcissistically* insist that the

seven letters are addressed to them are bound to miss their meaning" (116, italics added).

- " . . . such grammatical gyrations should cause our baloney detectors to go into red alert" (90).
- " . . . anyone who has read the Bible even once . . . " (119).
- " . . . a clear tip-off that you have just entered a spin zone" (129).
- "Prophecy pundits, however, were quick to spin the Scriptures in the direction of the spiritual realities on the ground" (184).

Concerning Tim LaHaye's view that Revelation 17 refers to the Roman Catholic Church, Hanegraaff says, "Bearing false witness is a serious matter" (124), indicating Tim LaHaye is lying.

Hanegraaff makes an unfortunate, lengthy comparison between Bill Clinton's testimony in the Monica Lewinsky matter and dispensational interpretation of the Bible. He says, "To interpret Scripture Clintonian style is to turn Scripture into a wax nose capable of being twisted any way the interpreter likes" (94). Is a comparison like this really helpful and appropriate in an intramural discussion? Why not just make your point and leave out the inflammatory illustrations? Hanegraaff only diminishes his own credibility with such statements. Moreover, this kind of comparison, like the comparison of J. N. Darby to Charles Darwin, throws an unnecessary obstacle in the pathway of meaningful dialogue, discussion, and mutual edification. This is not the kind of rhetoric that should characterize a debate involving a believer over an area that is not central to the gospel.

In this critique of *The Apocalypse Code*, we will focus our attention on three main areas—mistakes, method, and model. In the first section we will point out some mistakes in *The Apocalypse Code*. In the next section we will evaluate Hanegraaff's hermeneutical method and present what we believe is a more biblical, consistent method of interpretation. In the final section of the book, we will test Hanegraaff's method and his resulting model by examining several specific interpretations he sets forth. These will serve as test cases to enable you to evaluate for yourself which method and model is more biblical and consistent.

Hanegraaff claims to have discovered "the code to Revelation." Join us as we consider whether this claim is accurate.

## SOME PROMINENT DISPENSATIONALISTS

| | | |
|---|---|---|
| Thomas Spurgeon | Ray Stedman | Adrian Rogers |
| James Hall Brooks | Kay Arthur | David Jeremiah |
| Arno Gaebelein | Beth Moore | Charles Stanley |
| A. W. Pink | W. A. Criswell | Henry Morris |
| W. H. Griffith-Thomas | M. R. DeHaan | Billy Graham |
| Clarence Larkin | Lehman Strauss | Darrell Bock |
| William Newell | Chuck Swindoll | Charles Ryrie |
| Lewis Sperry Chafer | Jerry Falwell | J. Dwight Pentecost |
| C. I. Scofield | Chuck Smith | John F. Walvoord |
| H. A. Ironside | Greg Laurie | Tim LaHaye |
| Donald Grey Barnhouse | Skip Heitzig | Francis Schaeffer |
| J. Vernon McGee | John MacArthur | John Hagee |

# PART ONE

# MISTAKES

＊＋ ⚎✦⚎ ＋＊

As we begin this examination of *AC* (*The Apocalypse Code*), it is important to point out its errors. We did not include this chapter to nitpick *AC* or to try to "show up" its author. All authors know that any book can contain minor typos and misstatements. In hindsight, every author would probably like to change or re-phrase some wording in a book. Our intention is to simply point out statements we believe are inaccurate and to hopefully set the record straight on these issues.

＊＋ ⚎✦⚎ ＋＊

## CHAPTER one

# SEVEN ERRORS IN AC

──  ══✦══  ──

Error 1 *Hanegraaff, on multiple occasions, states in his book that no one held the pre-tribulation rapture before the nineteenth century. He says, "Prior to the nineteenth century, all Christians, futurists included, believed that a commonsense reading of Scripture inevitably led to the conclusion that the second coming/bodily return of Christ and the rapture/ resurrection of believers are simultaneous events."*[1]

In his diatribe against dispensationalism Hanegraaff singles out the pre-tribulation rapture for attack when he says, "For nineteen hundred years of church history, no one—including historical luminaries such as Ephraim, Augustine, Calvin, Luther, Knox, Zwingli, and Wesley— had any concept of the pre-tribulational rapture."[2] Hanegraaff is saying that no one until J. N. Darby in 1831 ever held to any form of a pre-tribulational view of the rapture.[3] Norman Geisler says, "As for the argument that prior to the nineteenth century all Christians were post-trib, even if it were true it would not prove anything. Even Hanegraaff agrees that only the Bible is the infallible basis for doctrine. So, ultimately the only thing that matters is what the Scriptures teach on this matter, not what the fathers said."[4]

We need to deal with the history of the rapture, not because it is the basis for determining truth, which can only be found in Scripture alone, but because this issue is consistently raised by critics of pre-tribulationism. Charles Ryrie has rightly said, "The fact that the church taught something in the first century does not make it true, and likewise if the church did not teach something until the twentieth century, it is not necessarily false."[5] Geisler notes that "heresies can be early, even in apostolic times (cf. 1 Tim. 4 and 1 Jn. 4), and (re)discovery of some truths can be later (like pre-trib)."[6] With this in mind, a careful study of church history shows that the pre-trib rapture position has strong historical precedent. It was not created by J. N. Darby in the 1830s as Hanegraaff maintains. There are several key voices from church history who held to the pre-trib position long before the 1830s.

What do we look for as we examine the historical record of the church in regard to pre-tribulationism? Rapture critic William Bell has formulated three criteria for establishing the validity of a historical citation regarding the rapture. If any of his three criteria are met, then he acknowledges such a reference is "of crucial importance, if found, whether by direct statement or clear inference." The criteria are as follows:

(1) Any mention that Christ's second coming was to consist of more than one phase, separated by an interval of years

(2) Any mention that Christ was to remove the church from the earth before the tribulation period

(3) Any reference to the resurrection of the just as being in two stages[7]

## The Shepherd of Hermas

An ancient writing known as *The Shepherd of Hermas* (ca. AD 140) speaks of a possible pre-tribulational concept of escaping the tribulation:

> **You have escaped from great tribulation on account of your faith, and because you did not doubt in the presence of such a beast. Go, therefore, and tell the elect of the Lord His mighty deeds, and say to them that this beast is a type of the great tribulation that is coming. If then ye prepare yourselves, and repent with all your heart, and turn to the Lord, it will be possible for you to escape it, if your heart be pure and spotless, and ye spend the rest of the days of your life in serving the Lord blamelessly.[8]**

## An Ancient End-Times Sermon

A clear statement of the pre-trib rapture position can be found as early as the fourth through seventh century AD. A sermon preached by Pseudo-Ephraem entitled *On the Last Times, the Antichrist, and the End of the World* or *Sermon on the End of the World* includes a concept very similar to the pre-trib rapture more than one thousand years before the writings of John Nelson Darby. The sermon is considered to be "one of the most interesting apocalyptic texts of the early Middle Ages."[9] The sermon contains just under

1,500 words. Concerning the timing of the rapture the sermon reads:

> We ought to understand thoroughly therefore, my brothers, what is imminent or overhanging …. Why therefore do we not reject every care of earthly actions and prepare ourselves for the meeting of the Lord Jesus Christ, so that He may *draw us from* the confusion, which overwhelms all the world? . . . For all the saints and elect of God are gathered together *before the tribulation*, which is to come, and are taken to the Lord, in order that they may not see at any time the confusion which overwhelms the world because of our sins (italics added).[10]

Pseudo-Ephraem clearly presents at least three important features found in modern pre-tribulationism:

(1) two distinct comings: the return of Christ to rapture the saints, followed later by Christ's Second Advent to the earth,

(2) a defined interval between the two comings, in this case three-and-one-half years, and

(3) a clear statement that Christ will remove the church from the world before the tribulation.[11]

The fact that Pseudo-Ephraem placed the rapture three and one-half years before the tribulation is not an argument for mid-tribulationism because it appears that for him the whole tribulation was only three-and-one-half years in duration. (Even J. N. Darby first believed that the rapture would occur three-and-one-half years before the second coming).[12] Therefore, we can assuredly say that the pre-trib rapture position is not a recent view. It was held and preached possibly as early as AD 373. The alleged novelty of this view should no longer be used as an argument against it.

Interestingly, Hanegraaff discusses the Pseudo-Ephraem text at some length and concludes that it doesn't support a pre-trib rapture. He then says that what Pseudo-Ephraem said about the rapture doesn't matter anyway because it's what the Bible says that really matters.[13] But if church history doesn't matter, then why does Hanegraaff even raise the issue of the lack of any support for the pre-trib rapture before 1830? One cannot have it both ways. You cannot argue church history to support your view and then turn around and discount it when you fear it may go against your view. Fairness requires an even-handed, balanced approach.

Further, Hanegraaff appears to favor the amillennial view of Christ's thousand-year reign (as opposed to our premillennial view) and favors preterism over our view of futurism as to the timing of prophetic fulfillment. "*The Code* ignores the more important issue of premillennialism which has abundant support in the early fathers," notes Geisler, "and if believing an early view eliminates its opposing view, then Hanegraaff's amill view is thereby eliminated."[14] Hanegraaff's amillennialism did not arise until the fifth century when Augustine developed it.[15] Even though futurism, which we hold to, is found and is dominant in the early church,[16] Hanegraaff's preterism only began to appear in its mildest form in the late sixteenth century.[17] Does this poison the well of Hanegraaff's views?

## Brother Dolcino

In AD 1260 a man named Gerard Sagarello founded a group known as the Apostolic Brethren in northern Italy. He founded this order after he was turned down for membership by the Franciscan order.

At that time it was against church law to form any new ecclesiastical order, so the Apostolic Brethren were subjected to severe persecution. In 1300, Gerard was burned at the stake, and a man named Brother Dolcino took over leadership of the movement. Under his hand, the order grew and eventually numbered in the thousands. End-time prophecy evidently held an important place in the study and teaching of the Apostolic Brethren.

Brother Dolcino died in 1307, and in 1316 an anonymous notary of the diocese of Vercelli in northern Italy wrote a brief treatise in Latin that set forth the deeds and beliefs of the Apostolic Brethren. This treatise was called *The History of Brother Dolcino*. Francis Gumerlock, a non-pre-tribulationist, is the individual who recently discovered the Brother Dolcino rapture teaching. Gumerlock says,

> **Again, [Dolcino believed and preached and taught] that within those three years Dolcino himself and his followers will preach the coming of the Antichrist. And that the Antichrist was coming into this world within the bounds of the said three-and-a-half years; and after he had come, then** *he [Dolcino] and his followers would*

*be transferred into paradise*, **in which are Enoch and Elijah. And in this way they will be** *preserved unharmed from the persecution of Antichrist.* **And that then Enoch and Elijah themselves would descend on the earth for the purpose of preaching [against] Antichrist. Then they would be killed by him or by his servants, and thus** *Antichrist would reign for a long time.* **But when the Antichrist is dead, Dolcino himself, who then would be the holy pope, and his preserved followers, will descend on the earth, and will preach the right faith of Christ to all, and will convert those who will be living then to the true faith of Jesus Christ.**[18]

Several points here are very similar to that of modern pre-tribulationism.

1   The Latin word *transferrentur*, meaning "they would be transferred," is the same word used by medieval Christians to describe the rapture of Enoch to heaven.

2   The subjects of this rapture were to be Brother Dolcino and his followers. This was not a partial rapture theory because Brother Dolcino considered the Apostolic Brethren to be the true church in contrast to the Roman Catholic Church.

3   The purpose of the rapture was to preserve the people from the persecution of the Antichrist.

4   The text presents the "transference" of believers to heaven and the "descent" of believers from heaven as two separate events.

5   The text also shows that quite a long gap of time must intervene between the rapture of the saints

to heaven and the return of the saints from heaven.[19]

Gumerlock clearly believes that this is a pre-trib rapture statement. He concludes:

> **This paragraph from** *The History of Brother Dolcino* **indicates that in northern Italy in the early fourteenth century a teaching very similar to modern pre-tribulationalism was being preached. Responding to distressing political and ecclesiastical conditions, Dolcino engaged in detailed speculations about eschatology and believed that the coming of the Antichrist was imminent. He also believed that the means by which God would protect His people from the persecution of the Antichrist would be through a translation of the saints to paradise.[20]**

The ancient witnesses presented thus far are enough to show that the pre-trib view is not a recent invention. But there is more.

## The Post-Reformation Church

By the late 1500s and the early 1600s, premillennialism began to return as a factor within the mainstream church after more than a thousand-year reign of amillennialism. With the flowering of biblical interpretation during the post-Reformation Period, premillennial interpreters began to abound throughout Protestantism and so did the development of sub-issues like the rapture.

Some claim it was the Puritans who separated the rapture from the second coming. Paul Boyer holds that Increase Mather proved "that the saints would 'be *caught up into the air'* beforehand, thereby escaping the final conflagration—an early formulation of the rapture doctrine more fully elaborated in the nineteenth century."[21] Whatever these men were saying, it is clear that the application of a more consistent, literal hermeneutic was leading to a distinction between the rapture and the second coming as separate events.

Others began to speak of the rapture. Paul Benware notes:

> Peter Jurieu in his book *Approaching Deliverance of the Church* (1687) taught that Christ would come in the air to rapture the saints and return to heaven before the battle of Armageddon. He spoke of a secret rapture prior to His coming in glory and judgment at Armageddon. Philip Doddridge's commentary on the New Testament (1738) and John Gill's commentary on the New Testament (1748) both use the term *rapture* and speak of it as imminent. It is clear that these men believed that this coming will precede Christ's descent to the earth and the time of judgment. The purpose was to preserve believers from the time of judgment. James Macknight (1763) and Thomas Scott (1792) taught that the righteous will be carried to heaven, where they will be secure until the time of judgment is over.[22]

Frank Marotta, a Brethren researcher, believes that Thomas Collier in 1674 made reference to a pretribulational rapture, but then rejected the view,[23] thus showing his awareness that such a view was being taught in the late seventeenth century. There is also the interesting case of John Asgill, who wrote a book in 1700 about the possibility of translation (i.e. rapture) without seeing death.[24] As a result of writing this book, Asgill was removed from the Irish parliament in 1703 and then from the English parliament in 1707. "His book had been examined and pronounced blasphemous, and had been burnt by order of the House without his having been heard in its defense."[25] Asgill spent the last thirty years of his life in prison because of his book on the rapture. This would tend to throw cold water on other early proponents of the rapture.

## Morgan Edwards

One of the clearest references to a pre-tribulation rapture before the time of J. N. Darby came from a Baptist named Morgan Edwards. He was the founder of the Ivy League school, Brown University. Edwards saw a distinct rapture three-and-a-half years before the start of the millennium. The teaching of Edwards, who wrote about his pre-trib beliefs in 1744 and later published them in 1788, is significant.

He taught the following about the rapture:

**II.** *The distance between the first and second resurrection will be somewhat more than a thousand years.*

I say, *somewhat more—,* **because the dead saints will be raised, and the living changed at Christ's "appearing in the air" (I Thess. iv. 17); and this will be about three years and a half before the *millennium,* as we shall see hereafter: but will he and they abide in the air all that time? No: they will ascend to paradise, or to some one of those many "mansions in the Father's house" (John xiv. 2), and disappear during the foresaid period of time.**

28

**The design of this retreat and disappearing will be to judge the risen and changed saints; for "now the time is come that judgment must begin," and that will be "at the house of God" (I Pet. iv. 17) (The spelling of all Edwards' quotes have been modernized; emphasis added).** [26]

Notice that Edwards makes three key points that are consistent with the pre-trib view.

1. He clearly separates the rapture from the second coming by three-and-a-half years.

2. He uses modern pre-trib rapture verses (1 Thessalonians 4:17 and John 14:2) to describe the rapture and support his view.

3. He believed the judgment seat of Christ (rewarding) for believers will occur in heaven while the tribulation is raging on earth.

The only difference between modern pre-tribulationism and Edwards' view is the time interval of three-and-a-half years between the rapture and the second coming, instead of seven. However, this does not mean that Edwards was a mid-tribulationist, since it appears that he believed the total length of the tribulation was three-and-a-half years.

The Morgan Edwards' pre-trib rapture statement is so clear that it was accepted even by John Bray who had to pay up on a $500 bet he made that no one could find a pre-trib statement before the 1800s. Such pre-Darby rapture discoveries are increasingly recognized by the scholarly world. Jonathan Burnham in his Ph.D. dissertation from Oxford University said, "Darby was certainly not the first theologian to advance pre-tribulational premillennialism. As a recent study has revealed, Morgan Edwards, the founder of Brown University in Rhode Island, has articulated the concept during the eighteenth century, well before Darby and contemporaries."[27] Tim LaHaye holds that,

> **For several years opponents of the pre-trib position have argued that it was invented by John Darby in the mid-1800s and was never mentioned before that. Quite simply, this argument is false—a fact that cost one post-trib writer a bundle of cash. This author offered five hundred dollars to anyone who could prove that the pre-trib rapture theory was known before John Darby began to popularize it in the 1840s. When it was discovered that the Reverend Morgan Edwards saw it back in 1744, the writer had to pay off his costly challenge. He has since had to admit his error and withdraw his offer.[28]**

## A French Connection?

Recently, British historian Timothy Stunt has made the case that Frenchmen also taught a two-staged coming of the Lord in a rapture. The two Catholics, Bernard Lambert (1738–1813) and Jean Agier (1748–1823) are said by Stunt to have taught a pre-trib rapture as early as the late 1700s. In fact, Stunt makes the case that Darby could have been influenced by these teachings before the Irvingites even formed. "While the Jesuit [Lacunza] sees Christ's return as one simple event at the beginning of the millennium," notes Stunt, "Lambert expects the event to be in two stages and foresees an intermediate coming when Christ first gathers His saints." "Agier

SEVEN ERRORS IN AC

also wrote of an intermediate coming in his earlier commentary on the Psalms (1809), he appears to have abandoned the idea after studying Lacunza's work."[29] Scottish scholar and historian, Crawford Gribben, also supports Stunt's claim concerning the French connection. "What is certain, therefore," summaries Gribben, "is that the idea of a two-stage second coming was circulating some time before Darby heard Margaret Macdonald's ecstatic utterance in autumn 1830."[30]

## Conclusion

The idea that the pre-trib rapture is a recent invention is a well-worn "straw man" argument. It simply is not historically accurate, and teachers like Hanegraaff should stop using it. Francis Gumerlock, a Latin scholar, has told me (Mark) over the phone and via email that he has three file drawers full of ancient antecedents to the pre-trib rapture, mainly from the Middle Ages. He simply has not had time to translate all of them yet. "*The Code* argues repeatedly that the pre-trib view should be rejected because it was late in appearing," notes Geisler; "however, heresies can be early, even in apostolic times (cf. 1 Tim. 4 and 1 Jn. 4), and (re)discovery of some truths can be later (like pre-trib). The final question is not whether the early fathers held it but whether the New Testament taught it."[31] A person may choose to reject the pre-trib rapture position on other grounds, but no rejection of this view should be based on the faulty, mistaken argument that it was invented in the 1830s by J. N. Darby. Hanegraaff is totally lacking on this point and has simply demonstrated his ignorance of recent scholarship on the matter, most likely because of a deep bias against pre-tribulationism.

# Error 2 *In three places in AC (25–27, 106, 229–230),*

*Hanegraaff discusses Matthew 26:63–65: "But Jesus kept silent. And the high priest said to Him, 'I adjure You by the living God, that You tell us whether You are the Christ, the Son of God.' Jesus said to him, 'You have said it yourself; nevertheless I tell you, hereafter you shall see the Son of Man sitting at the right hand of power, and coming on the clouds of heaven.'" Hanegraaff states that Jesus cannot be referring to His second coming here, but instead is referring to His "cloud coming" in judgment upon Jerusalem in AD 70. He also says,*

> **Finally, the "coming on the clouds" judgment metaphor was clearly not directed to a twenty-first century audience as LaHaye presumes. Rather, it was intended for Caiaphas and the first-century crowd that condemned Jesus to death. In the words of our Lord, "I say to all of *you*: In the future *you* will see the Son of Man sitting at the right hand of the Mighty One and coming on the clouds of heaven." (Matthew 26:64, italics his)**

*Hanegraaff emphasizes that "Caiaphas and the Jewish ruling council would see Christ coming with the clouds as Judge of earth and sky" (106).*

The problem with these statements by Hanegraaff is that the high priest Caiaphas was not alive in AD 70 to see the events surrounding the destruction of Jerusalem, nor were most of the other members of the ruling council that heard Jesus' words in AD 33. They did not see the events of AD 70. How do we know this?

In late 1990, a group of archaeologists discovered the family tomb of the high priest Caiaphas in Jerusalem. Within the tomb they found a magnificently decorated ossuary (bone) box inscribed with the name *Joseph bar Caiaphas.* The bones within the box are from a man about sixty years of age.[32] Joseph Caiaphas was the Jewish high priest from AD 18–36.[33] In keeping with Jewish law, Caiaphas had to be at least thirty years old when he assumed the high priesthood in AD 18, but was probably older. Assuming he was thirty when he began the priesthood and lived to be about sixty years old, then the latest date for Caiaphas' death would be AD 48, twenty-two years before the events of AD 70. So, Caiaphas did not live to see the events of AD 70 within his natural life. If Jesus meant that Caiaphas would see the events of AD 70, as Hanegraaff maintains, then Jesus was mistaken. Since this is not possible, Hanegraaff must be the one who is mistaken. We must look for another interpretation of this passage if we are to avoid making Jesus the author of a false prophecy.

In Matthew 26:63–65, Jesus is telling Caiaphas and the ruling council that He is the Son of Man written about in Daniel 7:13 who will come on the glory cloud to judge His enemies and establish His kingdom. He is telling them that they will not see Him again until His return as the undisputed King of the earth and sovereign Judge at the end of the age. He warned them that the One they judged unjustly will one day judge them justly. A majority of scholars from otherwise varying viewpoints agree upon this common view. A few of them are: D. A. Carson, John MacArthur, Leon Morris, Robert Mounce, William Hendriksen; and there are many others. [34]

In *AC* Hanegraaff urges believers to "recommit themselves to *faithful exegesis*—to mining what the Spirit has breathed into the Scriptures as opposed to superimposing our models onto the Scripture"[35] (italics his). However, in his zeal to find a first century fulfillment for this prophecy, which clearly refers to the judgment at the end of the age, Hanegraaff has imposed his own meaning upon the text rather than letting it speak for itself, and were his interpretation to stand, he would make Jesus the author of a false prophecy.

Error 3 *Hanegraaff notes that Revelation was written to the seven churches of Asia and says that these churches were "seven historical churches in the province of Asia about to face the full fury of the ancient Roman Beast."[36] Hanegraaff relates Nero to the Beast and believes that the seven churches in Asia were about to face the great Neronic persecution.*

The internal testimony of Revelation indicates there was at least some degree of persecution against

Christians in the province of Asia at the time it was written. John had been banished to Patmos for his faith in Christ (Revelation 1:9), and the church at Smyrna was warned of imminent imprisonment, which indicates a more widespread and organized threat (Revelation 2:10).[37] The death penalty was a real possibility because the believers at Smyrna were urged to be faithful to death. In fact, Antipas of Pergamum had already been martyred (Revelation 2:13). One could argue that the persecution at Smyrna was instigated by Jews (Revelation 2:9); however, the banishment of John and the execution of Antipas must have been carried out by the Romans since the right to banish and execute was reserved for Roman authorities alone. So there was some degree of local persecution when John wrote Revelation. However, there is almost universal agreement among scholars that Nero's persecution never reached beyond the city of Rome and its environs, much less all the way to Asia.[38] This view argues strongly against a mid-sixties date for the writing of Revelation and favors the mid-nineties date when we know that some persecution by Roman authorities was occurring under the Roman Emperor Domitian.[39]

The only trace of evidence that the Neronic persecution extended beyond Rome is in the account of Paulus Orosius.[40] However, he is a very late witness (early fifth century) that Guthrie says, "tends to make extravagant statements in other respects."[41] Hanegraaff's interpretation that the churches of Asia were facing persecution by Nero is simply contrary to the recorded geographical extent of Nero's persecution.

Error 4 *Hanegraaff says that dispensationalists believe that the one true God has two wives—a bride (the church) and a wife (Israel). He calls this "bizarre" and "blasphemous" (63–64): "It is bizarre . . . moreover, it is blasphemous to hold that the one God revealed in three persons has both a wife and a bride (64).*

Yes, the one God of the Bible reveals Israel as the wife of the Lord, or *Yahweh*, and the church as the bride of Christ. Dispensationalists did not invent out of whole cloth these motifs; they are ones used by God in the Bible itself. One would think that Hanegraaff, who repeatedly emphasizes symbols throughout his book, would understand the dynamics of symbolism when it occurs in Scripture. Yet, he fails to distinguish between Israel and the church on this matter. Here is where Hanegraaff's replacement theology manifests itself. According to his interpretation, Israel is merely a symbol for the people of God in the Old Testament. When Hanegraaff comes to the New Testament, the church supersedes Israel, once and for all. The church now becomes the people of God. In contrast, we believe that *Israel* always means Israel and only Israel, and the church always refers to the New Testament body of believers in this current age. Thus, since these entities are two different people groups in the Bible, apparently the Lord has decided to depict Israel as His wife and the church as Christ's bride.

These are clearly two different pictures presented by Scripture. A wife is one that is already married, while the bride presented in the New Testament is one that is engaged (betrothed) and awaiting marriage. Israel is pictured as a wife, indeed an unfaithful wife, throughout the Old Testament. Dispensationalist Arnold Fruchtenbaum has summarized the Old Testament picture of Israel as the wife of the Lord involving the following phases: (1) the marriage contract (Deut. 5:1–3; 6:10–15; 7:6–11; Ezek. 16:8), (2) the great adultery (Jer. 3:1–5; 31:32; Ezek. 16:15–34; Hosea 2:2–5), (3) the separation (Deut. 24:1; Isa. 50:1), (4) the divorce (Jer. 3:6–10), (5) the punishment (Jer. 3:11–18; Ezek. 16:35–43, 58–59; Hosea 2:6–13), (6) the remarriage with restored blessings (Isa. 54:1–8; 62:4–5; Jer. 31:31–34; Ezek. 16:60–63; Hosea 2:14–23).[42] "These, then, are the six stages of Israel's relationship as the wife of Jehovah . . . and today Israel is in her period of punishment," notes Fruchtenbaum. "However, there will yet come the time when Israel will be remarried, at her national regeneration, and be reunited to her God with all of her blessings restored."[43] Such an ending is what Hanegraaff ignores in his reading of the Bible.

In his book, Hanegraaff only rehearses the adulterous phase of Israel's history (with which we agree) and leaves the wife of the Lord in her wayward state. Instead of taking into account the whole counsel of God, which includes the remarriage and future blessing of a converted nation of Israel,[44] Hanegraaff replaces Israel with the church. He says, "In fact, before apostate Israel is judged, true Israel must be sealed."[45] Such a statement is the language of replacement theology or supersessionism, which teaches that God is finished with national Israel in history and has replaced her with the church. Nowhere in the Bible is the church ever called Israel, as Hanegraaff has done by naming the church as "true Israel." He goes against the Bible when he replaces Israel, whom he calls "the prostitute of Revelation"[46] and replaces her with the church, "the purified bride."[47] "The contrast between the purified bride and the prostituted bride could not be starker,"[48] he declares. Notice that Hanegraaff equivocates by calling Israel a bride when the Bible calls her a wife.

The New Testament calls the church the bride of Christ (Eph. 5:25–33), which is said to have been a mystery (a past secret part of God's eternal plan) (Eph. 5:32). The picture of the church as the bride of Christ is very different than the motif of the wife of the Lord. When we consider all of the New Testament passages regarding the relationship of the church as the bride of Christ, we see the picture "that the church is a betrothed bride that is not yet joined to her husband."[49] Fruchtenbaum presents them as follows: (1) the espousal (2 Cor. 11:2), (2) the process of sanctification or maturing of the bride (Eph. 5:25–27), (3) the marriage (Rev. 19:6–9), the eternal abode of the bride (Rev. 21:9–22:5).[50] "If one makes the wife of Jehovah and the bride of the Messiah one and the same, he is faced with numerous contradictions because of the different descriptions given," concludes Fruchtenbaum. "Only when one sees two separate entities, Israel as the wife of Jehovah and the church as the bride of Messiah, do all such contradictions vanish."[51] For example, Israel was married to the Lord at the exodus about 3,500 years ago, while the church

SEVEN ERRORS IN AC

as a bride is not yet married. The Bible lays out two different motifs for two different peoples of God.

God has a unique plan for Israel and her redemption, and He has a plan for the church as well. Both are true, which is why the Bible uses the two different metaphors to speak of each people of God. Hanegraaff's problem is that he misinterprets God's plan for Israel by subsuming it into God's plan for the church. When one reads and digests the entire book of Hosea, which uses the marriage metaphor to depict the Lord's relationship with Israel, he realizes that Israel comes back to the Lord at the end, and they live happily ever after. Look at what the Lord Himself says in Hosea about Israel:

> I will betroth you to Me forever; Yes, I will betroth you to Me in righteousness and in justice, in lovingkindness and in compassion, and I will betroth you to Me in faithfulness. Then you will know the LORD (2:19–20).

> And I will sow her for Myself in the land. I will also have compassion on her who had not obtained compassion, and I will say to those who were not My people, "You are My people!" And they will say, "Thou art my God!" (2:23).

A few verses later in Hosea chapter 3, the Lord provides further explanation of Israel's history as follows:

> For the sons of Israel will remain for many days without king or prince, without sacrifice or sacred pillar, and without ephod or household idols. Afterward the sons

39

BREAKING THE APOCALYPSE CODE

of Israel will return and seek the Lord their God and
David their king; and they will come trembling to the
Lord and to His goodness in the last days (3:4–5).

# Error 5 *In discussing the 144,000 in Revelation 7,*

*Hanegraaff says, "To begin with, ten of the twelve tribes lost*

*their national identity almost three thousand years ago in the*

*Assyrian exile."[52]*

Hanegraaff assumes that only the tribes of Judah
and Benjamin maintained their identity after the
Assyrian captivity in 722 BC. There are three biblical
passages that refute this notion. First, many scholars
maintain that when the Jews returned from the
seventy-year Babylonian captivity in 538 BC, "exiles
from a wide background of tribes, villages, and towns
returned."[53] This included people from the ten tribes
that Hanegraaff says lost their identity in 722 BC.

Secondly, we know that the tribe of Levi, which
was one of the ten tribes besides Judah and Benjamin,
was not lost. When the remnant returned to the land
in 538 BC, the Levites are specifically mentioned in
Ezra 1:4–6. The same was true in the days of Nehemiah
in about 440 BC (Nehemiah 7:43). While the tribe of
Levi is not mentioned in Revelation 7, the fact remains
that the tribe of Levi did not lose its national identity
in 722 BC.

Thirdly, even in the New Testament, people from
the ten tribes were still identifiable. For instance, in
Luke 2:36, Doctor Luke identifies Anna as a member

SEVEN ERRORS IN AC

of the tribe of Asher. If the ten northern tribes lost their identity in the Assyrian captivity in 722 BC, how did Luke know that Anna was from the tribe of Asher approximately 5 BC at the time of Christ's birth?

The bottom line is that these ten tribes are not, nor have they ever been, lost. Many of them have been dispersed, but not lost. God knows where every one of them is located. Geisler rightly notes that Hanegraaff's view "is an insult to the omniscience of God. Certainly He who names and numbers the stars (Isaiah 40:26) and will reconstruct the dispersed particles of our decayed bodies in the resurrection knows who those lost tribes are and how to regather them."[54]

# Error 6 *Another factual error by Hanegraaff is his*

*statement that Arthur James Balfour "was raised on a steady diet*

*of dispensationalism."*[55]

Lord Balfour was foreign secretary when the British government issued the Balfour Declaration, a statement in 1917 supporting the reestablishment of a Jewish state in Israel. Balfour was a Zionist, but his views were not based upon eschatology, let alone dispensationalism. His sister and biographer said the following:

**Balfour's interest in the Jews and their history was lifelong. It originated in the Old Testament training of his mother, and in his Scottish upbringing. As he grew up, his intellectual admiration and sympathy for**

certain aspects of Jewish philosophy and culture grew also, and the problem of the Jews in the modern world seemed to him of immense importance. He always talked eagerly on this, and I remember in childhood imbibing from him the idea that Christian religion and civilization owes to Judaism an immeasurable debt, shamefully ill repaid.[56]

Historian Barbara Tuckman tells us that Balfour was "not ardent but a skeptic, not a religious enthusiast but a philosophical pessimist . . . that Christian religion and civilization owes to Judaism an immeasurable debt, shamefully ill repaid."[57] Apparently Balfour's bent toward Zionism originates in the fact that his mother made him read through the entire Bible (out loud) about once a year when he was a boy.[58] His familiarity with the Old Testament is the source of his Zionism. Tuckman characterizes Balfour's view of the Jews as follows: "To him they were neither tools of the Christian millennium nor agents of a business imperialism, but simply exiles who should be given back, in payment of Christianity's 'immeasurable debt,' their homeland."[59] Balfour was hardly one influenced by dispensationalism as Hanegraaff would have his readers believe.

In fact, it is probable that none of the key Christian Zionists of the early twentieth century in Britain were influenced at all by dispensationalism. Most of the Christian Zionists in Britain at this time were usually members of the Church of England, which has never tolerated dispensationalism.[60] Once again, such a statement reveals Hanegraaff's fuzzy understanding of church history.

# Error 7 *Hanegraaff says Tim LaHaye is "unlike early dispensationalists, who believed that the Jews would be regathered in Palestine because of belief in their Redeemer."[61]*

Hanegraaff provides no documentation for this erroneous statement. J. N. Darby believed that the Jews would return to their land in unbelief. He says, "At the end of the age the same fact will be reproduced: the Jews—returned to their own land, though without being converted—will find themselves in connection with the fourth beast."[62] Historian David Rausch in his Ph.D. dissertation *Zionism Within Early American Fundamentalism 1878–1918* writes, "The Proto-Fundamentalist believed that the Jewish people would return to Palestine, the 'Promised Land,' without converting enmasse to Christianity."[63] Again of dispensationalists, Rausch says, "In their view, the Jewish people would return to the Holy Land in 'unbelief,' and the Holy Land would once again become a fruitful land."[64]

## Conclusion

Having clarified these preliminary issues, let's delve into the core of *AC*; that is, the interpretive method that Hanegraaff calls "exegetical eschatology" or "e squared." Let's see if Hanegraaff's "e squared" really squares with the Bible as a faithful method interpretation.

# PART TWO

# METHOD

Hank Hanegraaff says of *The Apocalypse Code* that it is primarily concerned with method. He appears proud to tell readers that his methodology is "called exegetical eschatology or e²,"[65] as if no one before had ever produced a view of eschatology from proper exegesis. Interestingly, for someone who claims such a deep commitment "to a proper *method* of biblical interpretation,"[66] it is stunning to realize that Hanegraaff's "method" is stated as principles, rather than as an actual method, like the historical-grammatical, contextual approach, for example. We will examine Hanegraaff's principles of interpretive methodology, as well as present the time-honored method of literal interpretation, which is also known as the historical-grammatical, contextual approach.

## CHAPTER two

# A CRITIQUE OF THE METHOD IN AC

Hanegraaff says, "I have organized the principles that are foundational to e² around the acronym LIGHTS."[67] The letters of the acronym LIGHTS stand for the following principles: *L* refers to the literal principle, *I* represents the illumination principle, *G* stands for the grammatical principle, *H* for the historical principle, *T* for the typology principle, and *S* is for the principle of scriptural synergy.[68] Let's briefly consider each of these points.

## Interpretive Methods or Theological Beliefs?

A major problem arises with Hanegraaff's interpretative method when one realizes that only half of his principles can even be classified as interpretive methods (method), the other three are best classified as theological beliefs (model). Hanegraaff holds that, "above all else I am deeply committed to a proper *method* of biblical interpretation rather than to any particular *model* of eschatology."[69] It is not hard to figure out that when one incorporates theological conclusions (or as Hanegraaff calls them, a model of eschatology) into one's method that it is impossible to take one's method seriously. This is what Hanegraaff has done in *AC*, as we shall see.

In *AC*, the LIGHTS acronym conveys the six principles that compose Hanegraaff's method for interpreting Bible prophecy. He writes a chapter explaining and demonstrating each principle. We will examine each principle in order to see if it constitutes a legitimate exegetical principle.

## *L* for the Literal Principle

As noted above, the first interpretive principle is *L* which refers to the literal principle. Hanegraaff explains, "Simply put, this means that we are to interpret the Word of God just as we interpret other forms of communication in the most obvious and natural sense. And when Scripture uses a metaphor or a figure of speech, we should interpret it accordingly."[70] As stated above, we are in full agreement with his statement as it stands. In fact, it is somewhat similar to a hermeneutical statement by dispensational scholar Charles Ryrie:

> The principle might also be called normal interpretation since the literal meaning of words is the normal approach to their understanding in all languages. It might also be designated plain interpretation so that no one receives the mistaken notion that the literal principle rules out figures of speech. Symbols, figures of speech and types are all interpreted plainly in this method and they are in no way contrary to literal interpretation. After all, the very existence of any meaning for a figure of speech depends on the reality of the literal meaning of the terms involved. Figures often make the meaning plainer, but it is the literal, normal, or plain meaning that they convey to the reader.[71]

Even though Hanegraaff and dispensationalists state a somewhat similar theory of interpretation at this point, the difference in its application and emphasis is like day and night. In fact, most of Hanegraaff's chapter on literal interpretation focuses on why prophecy should not be interpreted literally. It appears that Hanegraaff's greatest concern about literal interpretation is that Christians studying Bible prophecy might favor it. This he considers a great danger. "A literalistic method of interpretation often does as much violence to the text as does a spiritualized interpretation that empties the text of objective meaning," opines Hanegraaff. "A literal-at-all-costs method of interpretation is particularly troublesome when it comes to books of the Bible in which visionary imagery is the governing genre." He then concludes, "Interpreting apocalyptic imagery in a woodenly literal sense inevitably leads to absurdity."[72]

Hanegraaff's chapter is primarily a polemic against Tim LaHaye's application of literal interpretation, misrepresenting him as one who is a "wooden literalist" or a "literal-at-all-costs" interpreter, rather than a responsible literal interpreter. A "literalist" or "wooden literalist" does not recognize figures of speech, metaphors, or symbols in literature. Is this really true of dispensationalists in general and LaHaye in particular? Clearly not! LaHaye recognizes these literary features; however, he believes that they represent different referents than does Hanegraaff.

In his chapter on literal interpretation, Hanegraaff introduces "fantasy imagery."[73] "What is distinct about such fantasy images is that they do not correspond to anything in the real world,"[74] he declares. Then he concludes, "While fantasy images are unreal, they provide a realistic means by which to ponder reality."[75] How does Hanegraaff think that reality should be pondered? He says, "Figurative language requires readers to use their imagination to comprehend what the author is driving at. Such imaginative leaps are the rule rather than the exception in that virtually every genre of literature contains metaphorical language."[76] Examples he gives of fantasy images include: "an enormous red dragon with seven heads and ten horns" (Rev. 12:3), "locusts with human faces, women's hair, and lions' teeth" (Rev. 9:7), "and a beast that resembles a leopard with feet like a bear and a mouth like a lion" (Rev. 13:2).[77] How should these symbols be interpreted?

Contrary to Hanegraaff's admonition that we should employ "imaginative leaps," the author, in this case John, often tells the reader what he means. The first symbol that he mentions is the red dragon in Revelation 12:3. If one keeps reading, he will discover that John tells us who the red dragon of verse 3 symbolizes. Verse 9 explains, "The great dragon was thrown down, the serpent of old who is called the devil and Satan." In fact, this identification is repeated in Revelation 20:2 where the biblical text says of an angel, "he laid hold of the dragon, the serpent of old, who is the devil and Satan." How does letting the Bible explain itself, letting Scripture interpret Scripture, need our imaginative leaps to understand the meaning of a symbol?

50

The locusts of Revelation 9:7 are not identified by Hanegraaff in *AC*; therefore, we do not know what he imagined them to be. We, like almost all dispensational interpreters, believe that they are demonic beings, or fallen angels for the following reasons: These beings come from the bottomless pit (9:1), the being that releases them is a fallen star from heaven (likely a symbolic reference to Satan) (9:1), the agent that releases them has permission from God as depicted by the key (9:1), when the demonic locusts are released they darken the sun (9:2), the locusts came out of the smoke from hell (9:3), the locusts are said to assume the appearance described in verses 7–10, which fallen angels are capable of presenting; and their king is said to be "the angel of the abyss" and named Abaddon or Apollyon (9:11). This interpretation is based upon recognizing and interpreting figures of speech and symbols that are used to convey a literal meaning of a future historical event.

In Revelation 13:2 we see "a beast that resembles a leopard with feet like a bear and a mouth like a lion." Regardless of who that Beast depicts, it is clear that the Old Testament imagery from Daniel 7:1–8 comes into play, yet Hanegraaff, who speaks of the importance of using the Old Testament to help interpret Revelation, never mentions that part of Daniel. When we let Scripture interpret Scripture, it becomes clear that the leopard relates to the Greek Empire (Dan. 7:6), the bear relates to the Medo-Persian Empire (Dan. 7:5), the lion relates to the Babylonian Empire (Dan. 7:4). Robert Thomas tells us, "The combined strength and brutality of historical Babylon, Medo-Persia, and Greece is what will comprise the total character of this Beast."[78] In both Daniel and Revelation the prophets see the Beast arising out of the sea (i.e., the Gentile masses of humanity) (Dan. 7:1; Rev. 13:1). The two prophets see the same end-time figure known as the Beast, which is also called the "little horn" in Daniel (7:8). Both have ten horns (Dan. 7:7; Rev. 13:1) and both speak blasphemous things (Dan. 7:8; Rev. 13:1).

Such connections are not only suggested by dispensational interpreters. Scholars like G. K. Beale, whom Hanegraaff quotes approvingly a couple of times, sees the same connections between Revelation and the book of Daniel.[79] Beale, who holds an idealist view similar to Hanegraaff's, nevertheless explains that John's use of the imagery in Revelation 13:1–2 is "a creative reworking of Dan. 7:1–7."[80] Beale's identification of the Beast in Revelation 13 is one with which most dispensationalists would concur.

> **Whereas in Dan. 7:3–8 the lion, bear, leopard, and "terrifying" beast represent four successive world empires, in Rev. 13:1–2 these four images are applied to the one Beast. This probably includes a connotation of Rome as the fourth beast, which Daniel predicted would be more powerful and dreadful than the previous three beasts of Dan. 7:4–6 (see on Rev. 13:1 for specific allusions to Daniel's fourth kingdom). The combination of four beasts into one highlights the extreme fierceness of this Beast.[81]**

In spite of the above biblical support, *AC* takes a preterist view of the Beast and identifies him as

Nero, the Roman emperor who committed suicide in AD 68.[82]

Throughout his chapter on the literal principle of interpretation Hanegraaff fails to show how the literal interpretation of prophecy should be applied. Apparently he is too busy trying to make Tim LaHaye and other dispensationalists look as if they are unable to recognize and interpret figurative language and symbols. He accuses LaHaye of the following: "hyper-literalism" (20), a "literalistic approach" (20), and a "woodenly literal sense" (21). These descriptions are designed to make it appear that LaHaye and dispensationalists cannot recognize figures of speech and symbols as intended by the biblical author. This is clearly not the case. Dispensationalists do take the dragon, for instance, to be a symbol for Satan, and the Beast to be a symbol for the human antichrist. If we were really wooden literalists then we would think that the dragon and beast were actual animals. In reality the differences between Hanegraaff and LaHaye concern whom the symbols represent. *AC* advocates a preterist view, that these passages were fulfilled in the past, while dispensationalists believe that they will be fulfilled in the future since they have clearly not been fulfilled in past history. We also believe that instead of man's imaginary definitions of fantasy imagery, it is best to let the biblical text itself provide the identity of symbols.

## *I* for the Illumination Principle

*AC* teaches that the second interpretive principle is *I* for the illumination principle. We do not believe that this is a valid interpretive principle because, as Hanegraaff has correctly stated, interpretation is about method. The illuminating work of the Holy Spirit is simply not about method. Illumination is about the condition of a believer in Christ. Illumination is the work of the Holy Spirit within a believer, enabling him to understand God's Word. An unbeliever is blinded to the truth of God (2 Cor. 4:4) and does not welcome God's Word (1 Cor. 2:14); a believer, however, is able to see and understand God's truth (1 Cor. 2:9–3:2). This biblical teaching is not an interpretive method; perhaps that explains why there is very little in Hanegraaff's chapter concerning illumination.

It is very important that a believer has the illuminating work of the Holy Spirit in his life so that he will be in a spiritual condition with which to be receptive to God's Word. Illumination is a biblical doctrine that depicts a believer in Christ as one who has a light on in a room and can see what is going on, unlike the unbeliever who is spiritually blind to God's Word (2 Cor. 4:4). His mind is darkened and void of understanding (Rom. 1:21; Eph. 4:17–19). Illumination is not the same as inspiration. The writers of Scripture were inspired by the Holy Spirit to write God's Word (2 Pet. 1:19–21; 2 Tim. 3:16). Illumination, on the other hand, is the new state of a regenerate believer. John Calvin "insisted that the illumination of the Spirit was the necessary spiritual preparation for the interpreter of God's Word."[83] God may guide us providentially in our study of Scripture, but there is no spiritual inspiration in an illumined individual's study of the Bible.

## *G* for the Grammatical Principle

The third interpretive principle is the grammatical principle, that one should follow the rules of grammar when interpreting biblical literature. One should not come up with an interpretation that goes against the rules of grammar. Literal interpretation, which is what we use, is also known as the historical-grammatical, contextual method of interpretation.

One would think that this chapter in *AC* would provide an explanation of how and why grammar is important for correct interpretation of biblical prophecy, but such is not the case. In fact, the principles of grammar are rarely mentioned. Instead, Hanegraaff is preoccupied with the attempt to support his preterist views of the Olivet Discourse and the book of Revelation. Hanegraaff argues that only preterists interpret what he believes to be key words like "you," "this generation," "soon," and "near" in a grammatical and literal way. Such is not the case as will be demonstrated later in this book.[84] The point is, as dispensationalists we take a different literal interpretation of these items and none of our views are in conflict with the rules of grammar.

## *H* for the Historical Principle

Normally the historical principle in biblical interpretation relates to interpreting a passage according to a work's historical context. Not so in *AC*! Apparently, the historical principle provides an opportunity for Hanegraaff to speak out on a potpourri of hot button issues on eschatology and history. This chapter includes

Hanegraaff's understanding of when the book of Revelation was written, which is crucial for his preterist interpretation, as well as who wrote the Apocalypse (we agree with him that it was the apostle John). The date of Revelation's writing and a number of other historical items are dealt with later in this book.

## *T* for the Typology Principle

Hanegraaff describes his typology principle in *AC* as "persons, places, events, or things in redemptive history serve as types of Christ or spiritual realities pertaining to Christ."[85] Again, he says, "A type must therefore be a historical person, event, or institution that prefigures another reality in redemptive history, which is yet future."[86] "The greater reality to which a type points and in which it finds its fulfillment is referred to as an antitype," declares Hanegraaff. We agree with Roy Zuck, a professor of hermeneutics at Dallas Seminary, whose definition of typology is:

> **A type may be defined as an Old Testament person, event, or thing having historical reality and designed by God to prefigure (foreshadow) in a preparatory way a real person, event, or thing so designated in the New Testament and that corresponds to and fulfills (heightens) the type.**[87]

Even though Hanegraaff's formulation of types and antitypes has much to be commended, he misuses typology. When Hebrews 9:24 explains that the earthly temple rituals were copies or antitypes of ones in heaven, that does not mean the earthly ones were not actual or historical. However, Hanegraaff's primary use of his typology principle is to teach that the New Testament is a "greater reality" that supersedes or replaces Old Testament promises, especially ones relating to Israel, which is taught nowhere in the New Testament. In fact, his statement that the typology principle "adds to our understanding by underscoring that the mark of the Beast is simply a parody of the mark of the Lamb,"[88] does not even coincide with his belief that typology involves New Testament writers and their "typological interpretation of the Old Testament."[89] Both the mark of the Beast and the so-called "mark" of the Lamb are only in the New Testament.[90] "It is not too much to say," declares Hanegraaff, "that the biblical principle of typology is anathema for Christian Zionists such as Tim LaHaye."[91] We do not have any problems with the "biblical" principle of typology; however, Hanegraaff's misapplication goes beyond the biblical bounds.

Typology, like illumination, is not a primary aspect or principle of a method for exegesis—or "leading out" the meaning of Scripture; instead, as Paul says, some Old Testament events were types, patterns, illustrations, or examples to help us live the Christian life (1 Cor. 10:6, 11). After one has interpreted a passage historically and grammatically, then one can practice what in 1 Corinthians 10 Paul admonishes us to do. He instructs us to find patterns or examples from Old Testament events that encourage us in living for the Lord today. We agree that the New Testament authors have done that upon occasion (for example, Rom. 5:14; Heb. 8:5; 9:24; 10:1). However, to make typology a primary part of one's hermeneutic, as Hanegraaff does, is wrong. This is placing model where method should be. Typology is something that falls into the realm of application and not interpretation. But why should typology not be part of one's interpretative method?

When we read the Old Testament narrative in Genesis, it is clear that the life of Joseph, for example, unfolded as a real, historical event. The Bible does not record everything that happened in the life of Joseph, but only those events that relate to what God wants us to know and to that which is important to the flow of His revelation. Therefore, some patterns or events, when looked at from the New Testament perspective, foreshadow similar events in the life of Israel or Jesus the Messiah.

Examples from the life of Joseph that are types of Christ and Israel include: rejection by his Jewish brothers (Gen. 37:5–11), his brothers' plot to kill him (Gen. 37:18–24), his brothers' decision to sell him into slavery (Gen. 37:25–28), Joseph being accepted by the Gentiles (Gen. 41), Joseph revealing himself to his brothers (Gen. 45:1–15),—a type of Christ's end-time revelation of Himself to Israel—and their later conversion (Zech. 12:10–13:1).

There is no such thing in proper biblical interpretation as a specific biblical text that should first be interpreted typologically, as its primary or basic interpretation. All biblical texts must first be understood in their historical-grammatical contexts in order to observe a pattern of events which may then be applied typologically. However, Hanegraaff believes that the

"old covenant shadows find their final consummation in the person and work of Jesus Christ."[92] It is true
Old Testament shadows find fulfillment in Christ, but
Hanegraaff extends the scope of fulfillment beyond
what the New Testament intends.

Hanegraaff extends New Testament fulfillment
through his typology principle to include many of
the promises and prophecies made to Israel, especially concerning Jerusalem and the land of Israel.
Nowhere, however, does the Bible call these shadows
or types. "Christian Zionists," contends Hanegraaff,
"are convinced that these promises God made to
Abraham, Isaac, and Jacob with respect to the land are
unconditional and yet unfulfilled" (177). We do believe
this because nowhere does the Old or New Testament
teach that God has already fulfilled them, given them
instead to the church in some way, or that Christ in
the New Testament has changed the meaning of their
fulfillment. As Paul says, "And this is My covenant with
them [Israel], when I take away their sins . . . from the
standpoint of God's choice they [Israel] are beloved for
the sake of the fathers; for the gifts and the calling of
God are irrevocable" (Rom. 11:27–29).

Clearly Christ Jesus is the One through whom
the promises to Israel will be fulfilled, but typology
does not allow for Hanegraaff's brand of replacement
theology. He declares, "The land promises are fully and
finally fulfilled in the final future through Jesus who
leads the spiritual descendants of Abraham into Paradise restored .... The promise is typologically fulfilled
in the Lord."[93] We all agree that our ultimate destiny

BREAKING THE APOCALYPSE CODE

is that heavenly city (Heb. 12:22–24; Rev. 21–22), but in the meantime, history will also see the Lord faithfully and literally fulfilling all promises to Israel, which includes His land promises to her (Amos 9:13–15). Geisler has noted,

> **There is no biblical principle of typology that says the literal and unconditional Davidic throne and Abrahamic land promises are fulfilled in Christ, as** *The Code* **wrongly contends (224–225). There is no principle of typology that negates the land promises to Abraham's literal descendants "forever" by claiming that "the lesser is fulfilled and rendered obsolete by the greater" (201).** [94]

Hanegraaff uses his typology principle in a way the Bible does not justify and in an attempt to get his readers to believe that God is finished with national Israel. As a result, he goes where many have gone who do not see a biblical future for Israel, he has become an outspoken opponent of the modern state of Israel and an advocate of the Palestinian cause. Hank Hanegraaff is an advocate of Christian Palestinianism! [95] After all, vindication of Hanegraaff's theology depends upon God not fulfilling His promises to Israel.

## *S* for the Scriptural Synergy Principle

Hanegraaff defines his principle of scriptural synergy as a belief "that the whole of Scripture is greater than the sum of its individual passages . . . that individual Bible passages may never be interpreted in such a way as to conflict with the whole of Scripture." [96] Traditionally this is called the analogy of faith, that Scripture interprets Scripture. This also is a theological outcome, not a method. This principle also presupposes that one already properly understands the meaning of all of the other passages that are supposed to shed light upon the one in dispute. One must first interpret a passage based upon the historical-grammatical, contextual method in order to be able to compare it with another Scripture. Therefore, one cannot escape the essential task of first reading a passage in its own context before claiming to use other approaches.

One of the problems with Hanegraaff's interpretive approach, as demonstrated in *AC,* is that he seems to know before he has read a specific passage what it can or cannot mean. Too often he does not let the Bible tell him what it means. For example, Hanegraaff knows before reading a given text that 144,000 does not mean 144,000, and a thousand years does not mean a thousand years, "every tribe of the sons of Israel" actually refers to Gentile believers, and God no longer cares for Israel or Jerusalem. Somehow, when the Bible actually says these things and a reader takes it at its word then such people are characterized as advocates of "wooden literalism," "literalism," or "hyper-literalism." How does he know? He supposedly knows because to hold such views somehow places one at odds with orthodox Christianity. Yet he often ignores plain statements on many issues in the biblical text.

Hanegraaff tells his readers that scriptural synergy "means that the whole of Scripture is greater than the sum of its individual parts." This is a non-sensible claim that does not apply to any literature, let alone the Bible. How can the parts of the Bible be more than the totality of the Bible or the complete story? The entire Scripture is the whole counsel of the Word of God, as Paul told the Ephesian elders (Acts 20:27). Something may be complete or total, but it is irrational to say that the total of something is more than the total of it.

"Indeed," continues Hanegraaff, "scriptural synergy, or what the Reformers referred to as the 'analogy of faith,' may rightly be referred to as 'the primary rule of hermeneutics.'"[97] No Reformer's view of the "analogy of faith" would square with Hanegraaff's view of "scriptural synergy." We agree with the traditional meaning of the "analogy of faith," but it cannot be "the primary rule of hermeneutics" because one must first interpret a given passage and know its meaning before it can be classified and then be compared with other passages. Such an initial interpretation of a passage is crucial in order to know how to properly compare Scripture with Scripture.

The analogy of faith means that "no interpretation is acceptable if it is contrary to the general tenor of the rest of Scripture."[98] This was an important point emphasized by Luther, as Ramm tells us:

> The Bible was a world of its own and so Scripture interprets Scripture. At points where the Bible was obscure the Catholic referred to the unwritten tradition of the church. But Luther shut the interpreter up within the Bible and made the obscure passage yield to a clear passage. Much of Catholic exegesis was nothing more than studies in patristics.[99]

Luther's version of the analogy of faith was set against the Catholic practice of quoting those whom the church believed were orthodox in order to win the day in terms of the meaning of a given biblical passage.

Luther and subsequent Protestants taught that Scripture is self-contained and means that a primacy is placed on arguing from a specific text itself, which is why the received Protestant hermeneutic became the historical-grammatical, contextual approach. Calvin said, "It is the first business of an interpreter to let his author say what he does say, instead of attributing to him what we think he ought to say."[100] Yet constantly throughout *AC*, Hanegraaff overrides the clear meaning of a text by saying that to take such a view would go against Christian Orthodoxy—at least Hanegraaff's version of orthodoxy. That is not letting Scripture interpret Scripture. Instead it is a form of allegorical interpretation in that he often reads a foreign meaning into a specific text; his reason for doing so is that it supposedly coincides with orthodoxy. Ramm notes that Calvin "rejected arguments for very orthodox doctrines if the exegesis involved was unworthy."[101] This is how biblical interpretation should be, whether dealing with prophecy or any biblical passage. Too often Hanegraaff has misused his idea of "scriptural synergy" as a guise with which to reject the plain meaning of certain biblical passages.

Having examined Hanegraaff's LIGHTS principles, we move on to present various problems with his interpretive methodology.

## Method or Model?

Hanegraaff says that the purpose of his book is to help people develop a proper *method* of biblical interpretation, not to get them to embrace a particular *model* of eschatology.[102] The problem with this statement is that methods are not neutral when applied. The application of any method will inevitably result in particular interpretations of texts. This is clear in *AC*. Throughout the book, Hanegraaff applies his method to various biblical texts and always arrives at a particular interpretation which almost without exception strongly disagrees with a dispensationalist interpretation. Hanegraaff may not believe that he has a particular model he wants the reader to embrace, but it is clear that he does have a model he *does not* want the reader to embrace—futurism or dispensationalism. He has what we might call an *anti-model*, and that anti-model is dispensational pre-tribulationism. He attacks the premillennial, pre-tribulational view at every turn. If his book were not primarily a book against dispensationalism, then one would think he would include at least one place where his model leads to an interpretation that is consistent with this viewpoint. But he does not. This seems to betray his contention that it is all about method and not model.

Moreover, in spite of his insistence to the contrary, we see clearly that Hanegraaff does have a model. He believes that all of Revelation has been fulfilled except Revelation 20:7–21:22. That's a model. It's called partial preterism.[103] He believes that Jesus' Olivet Discourse in Matthew 24 was fulfilled in the events surrounding

AD 70. This too is consistent with the partial preterist approach. However, his handling of many of the symbols and images in Revelation and his belief that there are multiple patterns of fulfillment is also consistent with an idealist approach. So, Hanegraaff's model can be accurately referred to as a partial preterist/idealist in his interpretation of eschatological texts. We will call his model a preterist/idealist approach.

## The Classic Straw Man

Hanegraaff repeatedly falls into the trap of using straw man arguments. He assumes that dispensationalism is monolithic in its interpretation. While it is true that there are certain foundational truths that bind all dispensationalists together, we do not walk lock-step in every aspect. For instance, Hanegraaff cites Hal Lindsey, dispensational author of the most famous prophecy book ever written, *The Late Great Planet Earth* [104] and his view that the symbols in Revelation 9 refer to helicopters. We would agree with Hanegraaff that this is not a sensible interpretation in the context. He also notes that some dispensationalists view the seven churches in Revelation 2–3 as seven successive stages in church history. Yet, like us, many dispensationalists reject this interpretation. By painting all dispensationalists with a broad brush and "cherry picking" a few erroneous interpretations that some dispensationalists hold, Hanegraaff attempts to bring down the entire dispensational system of interpretation. While this kind of arguing adds some sizzle for those readers who are easily persuaded, this straw man form of argument is weak and not helpful in the discussion.

## "E squared" (Exegetical Eschatology) is Not New

While Hank may have coined the term "exegetical eschatology," and the "e squared" terminology, he certainly didn't invent biblical exegesis of eschatological texts. Dispensationalists like H. A. Ironside, Donald Grey Barnhouse, John Walvoord, and J. Vernon McGee were using literary, grammatical-historical principles of interpretation before Hanegraaff was born.

Virtually all trained Bible students and scholars employ the grammatical-historical method of interpretation to some extent. But they often reach very different interpretations. This is true in many other areas of biblical study, not just eschatology. For instance, scholars faithfully study the biblical text and some see the doctrine of eternal security while others do not. The same is true of the doctrine of sovereign election, issues surrounding water baptism, the cessation of certain spiritual gifts, the role of women in ministry, and on and on. The point is that employing a certain method does not guarantee a certain result. The issue is not that Hanegraaff uses exegesis and dispensationalists do not, but rather that many good Christians who study the Bible can use a similar method and reach very different conclusions. When this happens, believers should avoid demonizing one another and using condescending language. We must try to understand one another's point of view.

## Very Little EE in *AC*

Another methodological weakness in *AC* is that there is very little actual EE (exegesis of eschatological texts).

Hanegraaff's examples of the application of his method do not faithfully employ the very methods he cites. For example, he provides a fairly good definition of exegesis when he says, "*Exegesis* is the method by which a student seeks to uncover what an author intended his or her original audience to understand."[105] The English word *exegesis* comes from the Greek noun *exegesis* and means according to BDAG[106] "setting forth something in great detail, explanation, interpretation."[107] Since exegesis contains the *ek* preposition as a prefix and means "out of," it is common to explain exegesis as leading out the meaning from what a text says. Hanegraaff's definition of exegesis is very good, except for the last clause: "his or her original audience to understand." The goal of an interpreter of Scripture or of any literature should be to understand the single meaning of what an author intended by what he said. Whether or not an original audience would have understood one's words is a non-issue in relation to what an author meant by what he said. Since exegesis means to lead out the meaning of a text, it is related to the single meaning of what an author intended. Biblical scholar Walter Kaiser tells us, "Let it be clearly stated that the supreme rule of interpretation is to discover and to define exactly what the human writer had intended to express by the words he used as a result of receiving the revelation of God."[108]

In order to develop a proper method for exegetical eschatology, one must start with a proper view of exegesis. Once a proper method of exegesis is developed then it must be properly applied to specific biblical passages in order to reflect an accurate scriptural eschatology. Since

Hanegraaff has adopted an incorrect theory of exegesis and sometimes misapplies the correct theories that he does have, it should not be surprising that his view of eschatology also falls short of the biblical revelation.

We will attempt to demonstrate this point further as we look at particular interpretive issues later in this book. One thing is clear, even though Hanegraaff may have coined a label or two and developed an acronym, there is no doubt that he has not cornered the market on either exegesis (method) or eschatology (model).

three

# HOW SHOULD WE INTERPRET BIBLE PROPHECY?

— ⊨⊧ —

### THE GOLDEN RULE OF INTERPRETATION
#### by Dr. David L. Cooper

*When the plain sense of Scripture makes common sense, seek no*

*other sense; therefore, take every word at its primary, ordinary,*

*usual, literal meaning unless the facts of the immediate context,*

*studied in the light of related passages and axiomatic and*

*fundamental truths, indicate clearly otherwise.*[109]

Throughout *AC*, Hanegraaff is extremely critical of those who believe that prophecy should be interpreted literally. It is certainly true that those of us who believe in a dispensational, futurist view of the end times also advocate the use of literal interpretation, not just for Bible prophecy, but when studying any part of the entire Bible. In fact, Tim LaHaye has long championed Dr. Cooper's golden rule of biblical interpretation. "If you follow this rule, it is relatively easy to understand Scripture; if you ignore it, you will always be in error," declares LaHaye. "That is particularly true of the prophetic sections of Scripture."[110] However, critics like Hanegraaff have often distorted what we mean by literal interpretation of prophecy by falsely characterizing our views as "literalist," and "wooden literalist."

This matter of literal interpretation of prophecy is the most important issue that determines for individuals whether the *Left Behind* theology is true. Therefore, we will attempt to set the record straight concerning this most vital concern.

## Literal Interpretation Defined

The dictionary defines literal as "belonging to letters." It also says literal interpretation involves an approach "based on the actual words in their ordinary meaning . . . not going beyond the facts."[111] The mother of all dictionaries, *The Oxford English Dictionary* cites, "Pertaining to the 'letter' (of Scripture); the distinctive epithet of that sense or interpretation (of the text) which is obtained by taking its words in their natural or customary meaning and applying the ordinary rules of grammar; opposed to *mystical, allegorical*, etc."[112]

Literal interpretation of the Bible simply means to explain the original sense, or meaning, of the Bible according to the normal and customary usages of its language.[113] We practice this method through daily conversation with one another. How is it done? It can only be accomplished through the grammatical (according to the rules of grammar), historical (consistent with the historical setting of the passage), contextual (in accord with its context) method of interpretation.

Literal interpretation looks to the text, the actual words and phrases of a passage. Allegorical or non-literal interpretation imports an idea not found specifically in the text of a passage. Thus, the opposite of *literal* interpretation is *allegorical* interpretation. As Bernard Ramm in his classic and authoritative book on biblical interpretation said, "the 'literal' directly opposes the 'allegorical.'"[114]

## Literal Interpretation Illustrated

At this point in our discussion we are speaking of one's system of interpretation, or hermeneutics. We are not yet considering the proper approach to dissecting and analyzing chapters, paragraphs, sentences, phrases, or words in the Bible. We are currently talking about one's interpretive approach to the literature of Scripture.

For example, Isaiah 2:1–5 is a passage that many have interpreted allegorically instead of literally. As you read the passage below make a mental note of whom Isaiah is addressing. What does the text actually say?

**The word which Isaiah the son of Amos saw concerning Judah and Jerusalem.**

**Now it will come about that in the last days, the mountain of the house of the LORD will be established as the chief of the mountains, and will be raised above the hills; and all the nations will stream to it. And many peoples will come and say, "Come, let us go up to the mountain of the LORD, to the house of the God of Jacob; that He may teach us concerning His ways, and that we may walk in His paths." For the law will go forth**

from Zion, and the word of the LORD from Jerusalem. And He will judge between the nations, and will render decisions for many peoples; and they will hammer their swords into plowshares, and their spears into pruning hooks. Nation will not lift up sword against nation, and never again will they learn war. Come, house of Jacob, and let us walk in the light of the LORD.

The text of this passage addresses "Judah and Jerusalem" (verse 1), "Zion," "Jerusalem," (verse 3), "house of Jacob" (verse 5). Yet many allegorical interpreters read this passage and simply substitute "the church" for the aforementioned synonyms for Israel. Nowhere does the text say anything about the church. Those who read this passage and note that it is referring to historical Judah and Jerusalem are interpreting literally—that is, according to what the letters or words of the text actually say. Those who say that it refers to the church, or something similar, are interpreting allegorically—that is, importing an idea about the text when there is no basis for such a thought in the actual letters or words of the text.

Allegorical interpreters take phrases like "the mountain of the house of the LORD," "all the nations will stream to it," "many peoples," and "the house of the God of Jacob," and say that this passage is teaching the conversion of the Gentiles to the Christian faith and their ingathering into the Christian church.[115] Such an understanding is not found at all in this passage. Such ideas have to be imported from outside the text. When this is done it results in a non-literal, allegorical interpretation.

A literal interpretation of this passage is one that is given in the *Tim LaHaye Prophecy Study Bible* as follows:

> Isaiah envisions the Kingdom Age, when the nations of the world will come to the Holy City (Jerusalem) to learn the ways of God. Christ Himself is the Judge who will direct the affairs of nations, and peace shall prevail. Then the instruments of war and bloodshed will be refashioned into instruments of peace and prosperity.[116]

This interpretation is literal since it understands Jerusalem to refer to Jerusalem, and so on. The literal hermeneutic understands that the author says what he means and means what he says. This is what is meant by the system of literal interpretation, or hermeneutics.

## Grammatical-Historical Interpretation

Dispensational scholar, Charles Ryrie, an advocate of literal interpretation, notes that literal interpretation is the same as the grammatical-historical method of interpretation:

> It is sometimes called the principle of *grammatical-historical* interpretation since the meaning of each word is determined by grammatical and historical considerations. The principle might also be called *normal* interpretation since the literal meaning of words is the normal approach to their understanding in all languages. It might also be designated *plain* interpretation so that no one receives the mistaken notion that the literal principle rules out figures of speech.[117]

A breakdown of categories within the system of literal interpretation includes grammatical, historical, contextual, and semantic. Let us examine each of these categories more closely.

## *Grammatical*

The grammatical aspect of literal interpretation considers the impact that grammar plays on a passage. This means that a student of the text should correctly analyze the grammatical relationships of words, phrases, and sentences with one another. Literal interpreter Dr. Roy Zuck writes,

> When we speak of interpreting the Bible grammatically, we are referring to the process of seeking to determine its meaning by ascertaining four things: (a) the meaning of words (lexicology), (b) the form of words (morphology), (c) the function of words (parts of speech), and (d) the relationships of words (syntax).[118]

Dr. Zuck has been teaching biblical interpretation for many years at Dallas Theological Seminary, and we recommend his book, *Basic Bible Interpretation* as a great place to start for anyone interested in learning how to interpret the Bible. Dr. Zuck provides further amplification of the four areas noted above:

> In the meaning of words (lexicology), we are concerned with (a) etymology—how words are derived and developed, (b) usage—how words are used by the same and other authors, (c) synonyms and antonyms—how similar and opposite words are used, and (d) context— how words are used in various contexts.

In discussing the form of words (morphology) we are looking at how words are structured and how that affects their meaning. For example the word *eat* means something different from *ate*, though the same letters are used. The word *part* changes meaning when the letter *s* is added to it to make the word *parts*. The function of words (parts of speech) considers what the various forms do. These include attention to subjects, verbs, objects, nouns, and others, as will be discussed later. The relationships of words (syntax) are the way words are related or put together to form phrases, clauses, and sentences.[119]

Even though the grammatical aspect of literal interpretation is just one of a number of areas, it lets us know that any interpretation conflicting with grammar is invalid. Grammar is an important and foundational aspect of literal interpretation.

## *Historical*

Proper interpretation of the Bible means that the historical context must be taken into account. One must consider the historical setting and circumstances in which the books of the Bible were written. Dispensational scholar Dr. Tan explains:

The proper concept of the historical in Bible interpretation is to view the Scriptures as written during given ages and cultures. Applications may then be drawn which are relevant to our times. For instance, the subject of meat offered to idols can only be interpreted from the historical and cultural setting of New Testament times. Principles to be drawn are relevant to us today.[120]

## *Contextual*

"A passage taken out of context is a pretext." This slogan is certainly true! Yet, one of the most common mistakes made by those who are found to have misinterpreted a passage in the Bible is that of taking a verse out of its divinely ordered context. Even though a sentence may be taken from the Bible, it is not the Word of God if it is placed into a context which changes the meaning from that which God intended in its original context. Dr. Roy Zuck says,

> The context in which a given Scripture passage is written influences how that passage is to be understood. Context includes several things:
>
> • the verse(s) immediately before and after a passage
>
> • the paragraph and book in which the verses occur
>
> • the dispensation in which it was written
>
> • the message of the entire Bible
>
> • the historical-cultural environment of that time when it was written.[121]

An example of a passage often taken out of context is found in Proverbs 11:30, which says, "The fruit of the righteous is a tree of life, and he who is wise wins souls." This is sometimes used as a verse to advocate evangelism. We are all for anyone who preaches the gospel to the lost. But when studied in context, the wise one who wins souls is one who is able to draw others to oneself and teach them wisdom. Wisdom, as used in Proverbs, refers to skill in every day living. New Testament

76

Christian evangelism is nowhere to be found in the context. If this passage is taken out of its context in Proverbs and the phrase, "he who is wise wins souls," is placed by itself in a contemporary context, then it would be understandable that it could be thought to be a statement advocating evangelism. However, such a meaning is impossible in its original context.

### Semantic

The principles of literal interpretation recognize that a word or phrase can be used either plainly (denotative) or figuratively (connotative), just as in our own conversations today. For example, we might use plain speech to say, "He died yesterday" (denotative use of language). Or the same thing may be said in a more colorful way—"He kicked the bucket yesterday" (connotative use of language). Every word or phrase in every language is used in at least one of these two ways.

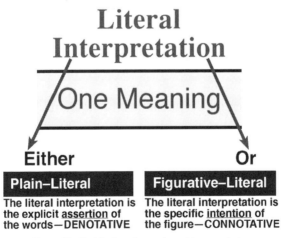

Created by Earl Radmacher and used by permission.

It is important to realize that even though we may use a figure of speech to refer to someone's death, we are using that figure to refer to an event that literally occurred. Some interpreters mistakenly think that just because a figure of speech may be used to describe an event (i.e. Jonah's experience in the belly of the great fish), that the event was not literal. Such is not the case.

Literal interpreters, for instance, understand that a figure of speech is employed by Isaiah 55:12. He is teaching that the Adamic curse upon nature will be reversed in the millennium: "And all the trees of the field will clap their hands." This figure is discerned by specific factors in the context in which it was written. Trees don't have hands and thus do not clap. This figure of speech relates to the removal of the curse upon nature at a future time. Such an interpretation is supported by the preceding and subsequent contexts surrounding verse 12. That this is a figure of speech is decided by factors within the text itself. If the decision about whether a tree can clap its hands was made on the basis of an idea imported from outside the text, then it would be an allegorical interpretation. Even though figurative language is employed, it will literally happen in future history.

Therefore, we see that within the interpretive process that the word *literal* is used in a second way, different from the first way in which we used it when referring to the system of *literal interpretation*. The second use of *literal* relates to the area or sphere of semantics and whether a word or phrase is used literally or figuratively. This distinction is important to note as later we will use it to reveal how Hanegraaff misrepresents the literal interpretation of prophecy. Dr. Ryrie drives this point home:

> Symbols, figures of speech and types are all interpreted plainly in this method and they are in no way contrary to literal interpretation. After all, the very existence of any meaning for a figure of speech depends on the reality of the literal meaning of the terms involved. Figures often make the meaning plainer, but it is the literal, normal, or plain meaning that they convey to the reader.[122]

Notice that figures of speech are not synonyms for allegorical interpretations. Therefore, a figure of speech in a passage does not justify allegorical interpretation. Remember, allegorical interpretation involves the importing of an idea, not actually stated by the words of the sentence, into a text. A figure of speech is simply a connotative expression made by the words or phrases within the text itself. An example of allegorical interpretation in *AC* is seen in Hanegraaff's equation of the 144,000 from all the tribes of Israel as including Gentile believers in general.[123]

## Literal vs. Literal

Dallas Seminary professor Elliot Johnson in his book on biblical interpretation notes that much of the confusion over literalism is removed when we understand the two ways it is used: "(1) the clear, plain sense of a word or phrase as over against a figurative use, and (2) a system that views the text as providing the basis of the true interpretation."[124] LaHaye and dispensationalists, by and large, use "literal" to refer to their *system* of interpretation (the consistent use of the grammatical-historical system), and once inside that system, in the area of semantics, *literal* refers to whether a specific word or phrase is used in its context figuratively or literally. Thus, literal interpreters considering semantics will discuss whether a word or phrase was meant by the biblical authors to convey a literal or figurative meaning.

## Hanegraaff's Shell Game

In *AC*, Hanegraaff uses a shell game to misrepresent and distort the literal interpretation of LaHaye and other dispensationalists. On the one hand, he attempts to make his point by arguing that since literal interpreters take some words and phrases as figures of speech, they are not consistent with literal interpretation. On the other hand, he says that we do not know how to properly understand figures of speech and symbols. Thus, Hanegraaff moves back and forth between the two connotations of literal in order to show that LaHaye and dispensationalists are irrational and mixed up when it comes to understanding Bible prophecy. Hanegraaff is playing a shell game with LaHaye and other dispensationalists as he moves between the two meanings of literal. As already noted, Hanegraaff often labels dispensationalists as ones practicing "literalism" or that we see figures of speech as "wooden literalists." Professor Bernard Ramm in his widely acclaimed book, *Protestant Biblical Interpretation* writes,

> The program of literal interpretation of Scripture does not overlook the figures of speech, the symbols, the types, the allegories that as a matter of fact are to be found in Holy Scripture. It is not a blind letterism nor a wooden literalism as is so often the accusation.[125]

## Literal vs. Allegorical

Why does Hanegraaff misrepresent and distort literal interpretation? If the literal interpretation of prophecy were left standing, he would have no basis for disagreeing with a dispensational view of the end times. Apparently Hanegraaff does not believe he would have a strong case against the dispensational view of Bible prophecy apart from distorting or misrepresenting the view.

In some of their more candid moments, opponents of literal interpretation admit that if our approach is followed, then it does rightly lead to the dispensational view. Amillennialist Floyd Hamilton declared the following:

> Now we must frankly admit that a literal interpretation of the Old Testament prophecies gives us just such a picture of an earthly reign of the Messiah as the premillennialist pictures. That was the kind of Messianic kingdom that the Jews of the time of Christ were looking for, on the basis of a literal interpretation of the Old Testament promises.[126]

In the same vein, Old Testament scholar Oswald Allis admits, "The Old Testament prophecies, if literally interpreted, cannot be regarded as having been yet fulfilled or as being capable of fulfillment in this present age."[127]

### Prophetic Fulfillment

One way that the literal interpretation of prophecy can be vindicated is by examining how past prophecies were fulfilled. Dispensationalist Paul Tan says that at "the first coming of Christ, over 300 prophecies were completely fulfilled." Tan concludes that, "every prophecy that has been fulfilled has been fulfilled literally. On the basis of New Testament attestations and the record of history, the fulfillment of Bible prophecy has always been literal."[128]

Ryrie also argues that the literal fulfillment of past prophecy means that future prophecy should be interpreted literally. He holds that "the prophecies in the Old Testament concerning the first coming of Christ—His birth, His rearing, His ministry, His death, His resurrection—were all fulfilled literally. That argues strongly for the literal method."[129]

As early as the book of Genesis, God demonstrates that prophecy is fulfilled literally even when figures of speech and symbols are employed. A number of dreams and visions are depicted throughout Genesis in which God shows the future to some of His people. A classic example is found in Joseph's dreams about his ascendancy over his family in Genesis 37:5–12. In both dreams God used symbols to convey the future. In one dream it was sheaves of grain that represented Joseph and his brothers, while in the other dream the sun represents Jacob, the moon stood for Rachel, and the stars were his brothers. Even though symbols and figures of speech occur, these dreams were literally fulfilled in the life of Joseph and his family as he later ruled over them when he rose to the second in command over Egypt.

## Jesus Breaks the Code

In his introduction, Hanegraaff sets forth "the real code breaker for the apocalypse," (xvii) which is "reading Scripture in light of Scripture," that is, consulting the Old Testament allusions in Revelation. Interestingly, there is no code to break! Revelation is not written in code; it communicates in normal language, which includes symbols and figures of speech.

Dispensationalists have long been on record as having recognized the importance of the Old Testament in the study of Revelation. Arnold Fruchtenbaum, a dispensationalist, has gone to the trouble of listing over 500 specific Old Testament references in the book of Revelation.[130] Fruchtenbaum's material has been out since 1977, but dispensationalists have always recognized the importance of the Old Testament in the study of Revelation.

It has been said that Revelation is "the Grand Central Station of the Bible because it's where all the trains of thought in the whole Bible come in." We agree wholeheartedly, and while he is correct in understanding the importance of the rest of the Bible in interpreting Revelation, Hanegraaff overlooks the built-in "decoder" found in Revelation itself. In Revelation 1, Jesus Himself establishes the pattern for interpreting the book's symbols. Jesus is pictured as the Son of Man (an allusion to Daniel 7) standing in the middle of seven golden lampstands, and with seven stars in His right hand. To understand this symbolism, we need look no further than chapter 1. Jesus provides the "built-in" interpretation, and also establishes a pattern

83

of interpretation for the rest of the symbols in the book. Jesus says in Revelation 1 that the seven candlesticks represent the seven churches and that the seven stars represent the seven messengers to the seven churches. By giving this built-in interpretation Jesus tells us two things. First, symbols in Revelation have a literal referent. Symbols refer to something that is literal. They are not symbols of nothing. Second, when we see a symbol in Revelation we should look first for a built-in interpretation in the immediate context. Often the meaning of a symbol will be revealed in the verses following it. There are at least twenty-six times the meanings of symbols are explained "in the book of Revelation itself either by direct reference or by implication."[131] Here are a few examples:

> The seven stars (1:16) represent seven angels (1:20).
>
> The seven lampstands (1:13) represent seven churches (1:20).
>
> The seven lamps of fire represent the sevenfold Spirit of God (4:5).
>
> The stars of heaven (12:4) refer to fallen angels (12:9).
>
> Satan is variously described as the great dragon, the old serpent, and the devil (12:9; 20:2).
>
> The waters (17:1) on which the woman sits represent the peoples of the world (17:15).
>
> Fine linen is symbolic of the righteous deeds of the saints (19:8).

The rider of the white horse (19:11–16, 19) is
clearly identified as Christ, the King of kings.[132]

The third thing Jesus teaches us in Revelation 1
is that numbers in Revelation are to be taken literally
unless specified otherwise. There are seven lampstands
and seven stars, and these correspond to seven literal
churches that existed in Asia and seven literal messengers of these churches. *Seven* means *seven* both times
it is used in Revelation 1.

## Conclusion

As we noted at the beginning of this chapter, the issue of
one's stand on the literal interpretation of prophecy will
determine whether one agrees with a dispensationalist
view of biblical prophecy. The late John Walvoord,
president of Dallas Theological Seminary for many
decades, put it this way:

> **The question of whether to interpret Scripture literally
> as opposed to non-literally is, therefore, a major
> controversy in the study of eschatology. Any student
> of prophetic Scripture must decide early whether
> prophecy should normally be understood by its literal
> meaning or in another way.[133]**

We believe the biblical text does indeed teach our
view of Bible prophecy. We believe that literal interpretation is the only valid way to interpret not only the
Bible, but all literature; and if that is the case, then it
follows that the dispensational view of the end times is
biblical after all.

## CHAPTER four

# SO WHAT? THE HISTORICAL IMPORTANCE OF METHODOLOGY

The well-known truism that ideas have consequences certainly applies to the issue of how to properly interpret Scripture, especially Bible prophecy. The book of Proverbs speaks of the end of a matter,[134] in other words, where does one's viewpoint lead? A good way to examine this issue is to see where interpretive methods have led in the past. We believe that Hanegraaff's interpretive approaches, if they become widely accepted, would send the church back to the Dark Ages hermeneutically. He may want to produce only a method of interpretation, but the moment anyone applies a method it produces an outcome or model of eschatology.

## HISTORY OF HERMENEUTICS

During the first two hundred years of the early church, two competing schools of interpretation arose. The Syrian School of Antioch championed a literal and historical interpretation, whereas a school in Alexandria, Egypt, advocated an allegorical or spiritual hermeneutic. Bernard Ramm says, "The Syrian school fought Origen in particular as the inventor of the allegorical method, and maintained the primacy of the literal and historical interpretation."[135] Alexander of Alexandria and Origen (185–254 BC) developed the allegorical approach to biblical interpretation in the early third century.

"The fundamental criticism of Origen, beginning during his own lifetime," notes Origen scholar Joseph Trigg, "was that he used allegorical interpretation to provide a specious justification for reinterpreting Christian doctrine in terms of Platonic philosophy."[136] Origen believed that "Proverbs 22:20 authorizes interpreters to seek a three-fold meaning in each passage of Scripture: fleshly, psychic and spiritual." Since Origen believed that "the spiritual meaning belongs to a higher order of ideas than the literal,"[137] he was attracted to the spiritual or allegorical meaning of the text. Scholar Ronald Diprose explains the implications of an allegorical interpretation as follows:

> He motivated this view by appealing to the principle of divine inspiration and by affirming that often statements made by the biblical writers are not literally true and that many events, presented as historical, are inherently impossible. Thus, only simple believers will limit themselves to the literal meaning of the text.[138]

Hanegraaff sounds just like a twenty-first century Origen when he exhibits just such a rationale. For example, Hanegraaff labels LaHaye's view of Revelation 14:20 as a "literal-at-all-costs method of interpretation," where the texts says that the blood from the slaughter will run 'up to the horses' bridles, for a distance of two hundred miles." He declares: "Interpreting apocalyptic imagery in a woodenly literal sense inevitably leads to absurdity." Why does he think this is the case? Hanegraaff explains: "Since it is difficult to imagine that the blood of Christ's enemies could create a literal river reaching as high as 'the horses' bridles for a distance of 1,600 stadia,' LaHaye exercises extraordinary literary license."[139] A page later Hanegraaff says, "Figurative language requires readers to use their imagination. Such imaginative leaps are the rule rather than the exception."[140] Hanegraaff imagines that the blood in this passage, rather than just emanating from the subjects of God's judgment, as the text says, is also a symbol "of blood that flowed from Immanuel's veins."[141] As his imagination continues to speculate, we find out that "the number sixteen hundred is pregnant with meaning." He quotes preterist commentator David Chilton who "explains, that the number sixteen hundred is a number that uniquely emphasizes Palestine. Four squared symbolizes the land and ten squared is emblematic of the largeness of the land."[142] How does he know that is what four squared, or sixteen hundred, refers to? Hanegraaff is clearly importing his meaning into the text. Where is the evidence that his explanation of sixteen hundred is the meaning? Why could it not be a multiple of eight, instead of four and ten? How does Hanegraaff know that these prophecies will not happen literally? We believe it will because that is what the text says.

The bottom line for the interpreters at the Syrian School at Antioch is their assertion that "the literal was plain-literal and figurative literal." By this, they meant that "a plain-literal sentence is a straightforward prose sentence with no figures of speech in it. 'The eye of the Lord is upon thee,' would be a figurative literal sentence."[143] Such an approach had a tremendous impact on Bible prophecy, and liberal commentator R. H. Charles notes: "the Alexandrians, who, under the influence of Hellenism and the traditional allegorical school of interpretation which came to a head in Philo, rejected the literal sense of the Apocalypse, and attached to it a spiritual significance only."[144]

Hanegraaff's downgrade of the modern state of Israel as prophetically significant also has roots in Origen and an allegorical hermeneutic. Diprose notes as follows:

> An attitude of contempt towards Israel had become the rule by Origen's time. The new element in his own view of Israel is his perception of them as "manifesting no elevation [of thought]". It follows that the interpreter must always posit a deeper or higher meaning for prophecies relating to Judea, Jerusalem, Israel, Judah and Jacob which, he affirms, are "not being understood by us in a 'carnal' sense."
>
> In Origen's understanding, the only positive function of *physical* Israel was that of being a type of *spiritual* Israel. The promises were not made to physical Israel because she was unworthy of them and incapable of understanding them. Thus, Origen effectively disinherits physical Israel.[145]

Hanegraaff's treatment of Israel follows the same course as Origen's. In Hanegraaff's model of eschatology, he clearly disinherits physical Israel and replaces her with what he regularly calls "spiritual Israel,"[146] which is the church. "Origen likens Israel to a divorced wife in whom an unseemly thing had been found," notes Diprose. Origen explains, "And a sign that she has received the bill of divorce is this, that Jerusalem was destroyed along with what they called the sanctuary."[147] Hanegraaff holds a similar view as he regularly depicts Israel "as an insatiable prostitute,"[148] while the church is "the purified bride."[149] In spite of all the evidence in his book, from a historical perspective, Hanegraaff says he has "never argued for replacement theology."[150] Geisler provides a more reasonable assessment when he says, "ideas do have consequences, and the typological-allegorical idea has had severe consequences in the history of the church. Denying a literal fulfillment of God's promises to Israel have led to anti-Semitism." Geisler concludes that those "who replace literal Israel with a spiritual church, nullify the literal land and throne promises, thus opening the door to liberalism and cultism."[151]

Although the Syrian school had great influence the first few centuries, the Alexandrian school eventually won out, as Jerome and Augustine were advocates of the allegorical approach in the area of Bible prophecy. Liberal historian Henry Preserved Smith concludes concerning Augustine that "with his endorsement allegory may fairly be said to have triumphed."[152] Their influence paved the way for the dominance of allegorical interpretation during much of the Middle Ages, especially when it came to Bible prophecy. Augustine developed a dual hermeneutic. On the one hand, he tended to interpret the Bible literally, but when it came to eschatology he interpreted that spiritually or allegorically.

## The Middle Ages

The Middle Ages was primarily dominated by an allegorical method of interpretation. Since Origen taught that the spiritual is the deeper or real meaning of a text, why deal with the inferior literal meaning of a passage when one can see so much more in the spiritual realm? One dominant late-medieval belief was that every sentence in the pages of Scripture has to be understood as referring to Christ. This erroneous interpretive dictum was based upon a misapplication of Luke 24:44, which says, "Now He said to them, 'These are My words which I spoke to you while I was still with you, that all things which are written about Me in the Law of Moses and the Prophets and the Psalms must be fulfilled.'" This passage does not say that every word or sentence in the Old Testament has to refer to Jesus, the Messiah, but instead that Jesus is the One being referenced in the Old Testament when it speaks of the Messiah. This would mean that a clearly historical passage like 1 Chronicles 26:18, which says, "At the Parbar on the west there were four at the highway and two at the Parbar," would have to be interpreted as referring to Christ. This sentence is not speaking about Christ, but through allegorical alchemy it was explained in some kind of Christological way. "During these nine centuries we find very little except the 'glimmerings and decays' of patristic exposition," notes Farrar. "Much of the learning which still continued to exist was devoted to something which was meant for exegesis, yet not one writer in hundreds showed any true conception of what exegesis really implies."[153]

## The Reformation

It was not until the dawning of the Reformation that biblical interpretation began to return to the sanity of literal interpretation. The Reformation could not have occurred if the reformers did not have the confidence that they knew what God's Word was saying. "The tradition of the Syrian School . . . became the essential hermeneutical theory of the Reformers."[154] Ramm points out that in Europe "there was a hermeneutical Reformation which preceded the ecclesiastical Reformation."[155] Thus, we see demonstrated once again in history that an interpretive method precedes and produces an exegesis, and finally a theological belief (i.e., model). Luther and Calvin generally returned the church to literal interpretation. Had they not done this, then Protestantism would have never been born and reformation would have never taken place. Luther said, "The literal sense of Scripture alone is the whole essence of faith and of Christian theology."[156] Calvin said, "It is the first business of an interpreter to let his author say what he does, instead of attributing to him what we think he ought to say."[157] However, like most of us, Luther and Calvin did not always follow their own theory, but they and like-minded reformers turned the hermeneutical tide in the right direction.

## The Post-Reformation

During the post-Reformation period many Protestants slowly cast off a thousand years of allegorical interpretation. They applied literal interpretation first in issues relating to the doctrine of salvation and then began to apply it to the entire Bible. Then, in the early 1600s there was a return to premillennialism as some started applying the literal hermeneutic to Revelation 20.[158] At the same time many Protestants began to see that there was a literal future for national Israel,[159] which was spearheaded by reading the premillennialism of the early church fathers[160] and for the English-speaking world the notes in the Geneva Bible.[161]

Even though literal interpretation was being restored during the Reformation and post-Reformation periods, it still took a while for biblical interpreters to more consistently rid themselves of the medieval allegorical influences. For the influential Puritan theologian William Perkins, "the medieval four-fold sense was reduced to a two-fold or double-literal sense."[162] This would be similar to Augustine's dual hermeneutic. However, most Protestant Bible interpreters were increasingly moving toward the literal hermeneutic and functioning within that framework so that the historical-grammatical, contextual method is labeled the Protestant hermeneutic.[163]

By the 1600s most biblical scholars preferred a literal interpretation; nevertheless, a couple hundred years passed before that understanding influenced all areas of Bible interpretation, especially Bible prophecy. Even though premillennialism had been restored, it was still dominated, to a large extent, by the blend of literal and allegorical interpretation known as historicism, which calculated time within a contrived day/year theory. To them, when the Bible cites 1,260 days from Daniel and Revelation, it really means 1,260 years. This is not literal interpretation!

It was not until the late 1700s and early 1800s that biblical interpreters grew more consistent in applying a literal hermeneutic. Wallis tells us that, "a consistent futurism, which completely removes the necessity for calculating the times, did not emerge until the early nineteenth century."[164] In general, the evangelical church, especially in the English-speaking world, returned to the premillennial futurism of the early church. Now they would apply the literal method and develop it beyond the beginning stage of the early church. As theologian Wilber Wallis notes, the views of post-Apostolic father Irenaeus (c. 185) contained the basics of the literal and futurist understanding of Bible prophecy as seen in modern dispensationalism.[165] The important point to note here is that as interpreters became more consistent in applying a literal hermeneutic to the entire Bible, especially to biblical prophecy; it undoubtedly yielded a futurist view of prophecy. "We have returned to Irenaeus' conception of the futurity of Daniel's seventieth week,"[166] says Wallis.

## IMPLICATIONS FOR TODAY

Hanegraaff admits to the current dominance of the futurist emphasis among Bible-believing evangelicals toward literal interpretation for the entire Bible including prophecy, but he wants to change this two-hundred-year trend. In fact, he wants to create a paradigm shift away from the literal interpretation of Bible prophecy and back toward the mysticism of the Alexandrian school and the hermeneutical trends of the Middle Ages. This is not progress, but a retrogression and downgrade of the interpretive process.

A shift toward the interpretive trend of the Middle Ages would have modern-day consequences. Beryl Smalley, a scholar specializing in medieval views of biblical interpretation, tells us that "they subordinated scholarship meanwhile to mysticism and to propaganda."[167] "Again the crisis was reflected in biblical studies. The speculation of Joachim signified a new wave of mysticism."[168] "Revolution and uncertainty have discouraged biblical scholarship in the past and stimulated more subjective modes of interpretation," she contends. "Conditions today are giving rise to a certain sympathy with the allegorists. We have a spate of studies on medieval 'spirituality.'"[169] Hanegraaff demonstrates in his *AC* that he is following the overall trends of both secular society and too many evangelicals who are moving away from literal interpretation into the shadowy darkness of non-literal hermeneutics.

We have also noticed how culture cycles between rationalism and mysticism over the years. Since the 1960s, American culture has definitely moved in the direction of and is now firmly dominated by a mystical worldview. However, biblical Christianity is not based on reason or mysticism as its starting point for truth; instead it is built upon revelation or God's Word. When mysticism dominates a culture's mindset, it predisposes one hermeneutically toward mysticism and non-literal interpretation. It is into this American evangelical climate that Hanegraaff's non-literal approach to Bible prophecy enters.

Dr. John Walvoord was asked a few years ago, "What do you predict will be the most significant theological issues over the next ten years?" His answer includes the following: "The hermeneutical problem of not interpreting the Bible literally, especially the prophetic areas. The church today is engulfed in the idea that one cannot interpret prophecy literally."[170]

Veteran evangelical scholar Walt Kaiser suggested about twenty-five years ago that the church is "now going through a hermeneutical crisis, perhaps as significant in its importance and outcome as that of the Reformation."[171] He notes, "The meaning of the text lies in its subject matter, rather than in what an author meant by that text."[172] Kaiser explains further:

> **The process of exegesis of a text is no longer linear but circular—one in which the interpreter affects his text as much as the text (in its subject matter) somehow affects the interpreter as well. Clearly, there is a confusion of ontology with epistemology, the subject with the object, the "thereness" of the propositions of the text with the total cultural and interpretive "baggage" of the interpreter.**[173]

Geisler says that his chief concern about the *AC* is that it "is based on an allegorical method of interpreting prophetic Scripture, that if applied to other teachings of Scripture, would undermine the salvation essentials of the Christian faith."[174] We share Geisler's concern, especially in light of the fact that it is this method that Hanegraaff wants to emphasize.[175] It is clear from 2,000 years of church history that if we do indeed adopt Hanegraaff's method for interpreting Bible prophecy, then it will put us back on the road to the subjectivism and mysticism of the Dark Ages. "It is sad that a man who has fought so hard for so long against cults and aberrant teachings," concludes Geisler, "has himself succumbed to a method of interpreting the Bible that is not significantly different from those used by the cults which he so vigorously opposes."[176]

# PART THREE

# MODEL

⊷⊷ ⊯♦⊠ ⊷⊷

Hanegraaff strenuously insists that his purpose in *AC* is to set forth a method of interpretation and not a particular model of eschatology (3). Unlike Hanegraaff, we recognize that method applied inescapably, necessarily leads to outcome or model. Also, unlike Hanegraaff, we aren't afraid to identify what our model is because we believe our model can survive scriptural scrutiny.

As we have seen, the principles in his method are not really new. The only new element is the "e squared" terminology. Likewise, the interpretations that come out of his method really are not new either. His model (yes, he does have one) is consistent with partial preterist/idealist interpretation. Hanegraaff, who consistently labels others on his program, is very reticent for some reason to have his theological interpretations identified.

In the next eight chapters, we have selected a few of Hanegraaff's interpretations in order to test if they are based on sound exegetical principles. These eight hermeneutical "test cases" will allow you to see our method of interpretation in action. You can then judge our model against his, side-by-side. You can put them to the test. We welcome the interaction.

CHAPTER five

# WILL THE ANTICHRIST DIE AND COME BACK TO LIFE?

— ⊷❖⊶ —

Let's begin these test cases with Hanegraaff's first application of his model in *AC*. The specific biblical text is Revelation 13:3–4.

*And I saw one of his heads as if it had been slain, and his fatal wound was healed. And the whole earth was amazed and followed after the Beast; and they worshiped the dragon, because he gave his authority to the Beast; and they worshiped the Beast, saying, "Who is like the Beast, and who is able to wage war with him?"*

In *The Indwelling* Tim LaHaye and Jerry Jenkins depict the Beast of Revelation (also known as the Antichrist) as one who literally dies and comes back to life.[177] LaHaye and Jenkins present the events of Revelation 13 as a resurrection of the satanic Beast. Is this really what the text of Scripture means?

Hanegraaff deems it preposterous, saying,

**If Antichrist could rise from the dead and control the earth and sky as LaHaye contends, Christianity would lose the basis for believing that Christ's resurrection**

vindicated His claim to deity. In a Christian worldview, Satan can parody the work of Christ through "all kinds of counterfeit miracles, signs and wonders" (2 Thessalonians 2:9), but he cannot perform the truly miraculous as Christ did. If Satan possesses the creative power of God, he could have masqueraded as the resurrected Christ. Moreover, the notion that Satan can perform acts that are indistinguishable from genuine miracles suggests a dualistic worldview in which God and Satan are equal powers competing for dominance. [178]

Hanegraaff said concerning this issue: "What is at stake here is nothing less than the deity and resurrection of Christ. In a Christian worldview, only God has the power to raise the dead." [179]

Has Hanegraaff accurately represented what Tim LaHaye believes? Well, . . . yes and no. LaHaye does believe the Beast of Revelation will be killed and resurrected. "As far as I know," declares LaHaye in his nonfiction commentary on Revelation, "this will be the first time that Satan has ever been able to raise the dead." [180] However, many of the conclusions that Hanegraaff draws about this are not what LaHaye actually believes.

## HANEGRAAFF'S FALSE PORTRAIT

Clearly, Hanegraaff has framed LaHaye's belief about the resurrection of the Beast during the tribulation within a context that LaHaye does not believe. How is "the deity and resurrection of Christ" at stake within LaHaye's understanding of the resurrection of the Beast during the tribulation? This is mere assertion on

Hanegraaff's part. He has apparently made no effort to find out exactly what kind of theological framework LaHaye had in mind on this matter. LaHaye's mindset is easily discovered by consulting his commentary on Revelation that has been in print since 1973. Far from the idea that "Satan possesses the creative power of God," as stated by Hanegraaff, LaHaye speaks clearly on this matter as follows:

> **As far as I know, this will be the first time that Satan has ever been able to raise the dead. His power and control of man is limited by God, but according to His wise providence He will permit Satan on this one occasion to have the power to raise the dead. When studied in the light of 2 Thessalonians 2, it may well be the tool he will use to deceive men.**[181]

LaHaye clearly believes that the resurrection of the Beast will be a one-time event, under the sovereign control of God and in no way "suggests a dualistic worldview in which God and Satan are equal powers competing for dominance." Hanegraaff erroneously presents LaHaye's view as if he thinks that Satan is autonomous and not under the sovereign thumb of our omnipotent God. It is obvious that Hanegraaff disagrees with LaHaye's futurist understanding of Revelation, but that does not justify his exaggeration of the end result of a literal approach to Revelation.

Why does Hanegraaff blur LaHaye's view? He claims that "the point is to demonstrate the dangers inherent in the interpretive method they and other dispensationalists employ."[182] The problem does not

BREAKING THE APOCALYPSE CODE

lie in the dispensational interpretative method but in those like Hanegraaff who do not fairly represent the views of others. Perhaps he must exaggerate the implications of others' views to generate the concern he thinks appropriate. Hanegraaff often quotes the famous maxim: "In essentials, unity; in nonessentials, liberty; in all things, charity."[183] So where is the liberty and charity in practice that he advocates in theory?

Hanegraaff is concerned that if these satanic deeds are in fact genuine, then "Christianity would lose the basis for believing that Christ's resurrection vindicates His claim to deity." Gregory Harris, a professor at Master's Theological Seminary, argues just the opposite since "exactly the same words used for the miracles of Christ and the apostles are used in reference to the miracles of the tribulation." He says: "To say that the signs, wonders, and mighty deeds attributed to Satan's forces will only seem to be miraculous could lead to questioning the veracity of the miracles of Christ, since one could say that they too only seemed to be miraculous."[184] This would mean that if the satanic exploits of the tribulation are not genuine miracles, but only sleight of hand, and since these exact terms are the very ones used to describe the miracles of Christ and the apostles (more on this later), then one could also legitimately say that the miracles of Christ and His apostles are not genuine, if we follow Hanegraaff's logic.

## Parody or Reality?

Is the resurrection of the Beast during the tribulation something that actually occurs or is it just a cheap trick?

Hanegraaff says, "Satan can *parody* the work of Christ through 'all kinds of counterfeit miracles, signs and wonders' (2 Thessalonians 2:9), but he cannot literally do what Christ did—namely, raise himself from the dead."[185] There are many dispensationalists who would agree with Hanegraaff's notion that the satanic trio (the Dragon, the Beast, and the False Prophet) do not perform actual miracles but only appear to do such through sleight of hand. On the other hand, as will be demonstrated later, there are a significant number of non-dispensationalists down through the history of the church who agree with LaHaye's position. Thus, it is wrong for Hanegraaff to present this as if all the dispensationalists are on one side of this issue, while all of the non-dispensationalists are on the other.

We believe that the "signs, wonders and miracles" done through satanic agency are indeed miraculous. Jesus (Matt. 24:4–5, 11, 24), Paul (2 Thess. 2:9), and John (Rev. 13:13–15; 16:13–14; 19:20) all describe miraculous works accomplished by Satan. The same language is used for miracles performed by Jesus, as will be shown later. "Is it possible that God will grant for a limited time powers that up to now He has reserved for Himself and His select agents?" questions Harris, "Since the tribulation is presented as unique from any previous time in history, should not unparalleled satanic power be expected, power he has previously been restrained from producing?"[186]

The point is that God the Holy Spirit is now restraining "the man of lawlessness" (2 Thess. 2:3) from certain activity during the current era (2 Thess.

2:6–7). Once the Holy Spirit steps aside, it will result in greater satanic activity during the tribulation: "the one whose coming is in accord with the activity of Satan, with all power and signs and false wonders" (2 Thess. 2:9). In fact, Paul specifically says of this activity during the tribulation that it is something God will send (2 Thess. 2:10). The purpose is "so that they might believe what is false, in order that they all may be judged who did not believe the truth, but took pleasure in wickedness" (2 Thess. 2:10–11). Next, we will consider why it appears that the Beast of Revelation will rise from the dead and do genuine miracles during the tribulation.

## Vocabulary

The primary language used to describe the miracles of Christ and the apostles are the terms "signs," "wonders," and "miracles." The Greek word for sign is *semeion* and means "sign" or "distinguishing mark" by which something is known. It is used of miracles by Christ and the apostles in many passages (Matt. 12:38; 16:1, 4; Mark 8:11, 12; 16:17, 20; Luke 11:16, 29; 23:8; John 2:11, 18, 23; 3:2; 4:48, 54; 6:2, 14, 26, 20; 7:31; 9:16; Acts 2:22, 43; 4:16, 30; 5:12; 6:8; 7:36; 14:3; 15:12; Rom. 15:19; 1 Cor. 1:22; 2 Cor. 12:12; Heb. 2:4).[187] This is the most common word used to describe the miraculous works of Christ and His apostles.

Miracles in the New Testament are also referred to by the Greek word *teras*, which is translated as "a wonder, marvel."[188] The noun "wonder" occurs sixteen times in the New Testament and is always coupled with the word "sign" (Matt. 24:24; Mark 13:22; John

4:48; Acts 2:19, 22, 43; 4:30; 5:12; 6:8; 7:36; 14:3; 15:12; Rom. 15:19; 2 Cor. 12:12; 2 Thess. 2:9; Heb. 2:4). All but 2 Thessalonians 2:9 describes the miracles done by Christ and the apostles and notes "something so strange as to cause it to be 'watched' or 'observed.'"[189]

The remaining Greek words used for miracle are *dunamis* and *energeia*, which are usually translated as "miracle" and "working." "Both point more to the supernatural source rather than to what is produced,"[190] concludes Harris. Other than in 2 Thessalonians 2:9, these words always refer to "the workings of God."[191]Amillennial Bible scholar Philip Edgcumbe Hughes ties it all together with the following statement:

> It is best to take signs, wonders, and miracles as belonging together rather than as indicating three different forms of manifestation .... Thus a sign, which is the word consistently used in the fourth gospel for the miraculous works of Christ, indicates that the event is not an empty ostentation of power, but is significant in that, signwise, it points beyond itself to the reality of the mighty hand of God in operation. A wonder is an event which, because of its superhuman character, excites awe and amazement on the part of the beholder. A miracle (or literally power) emphasizes the dynamic character of the event, with particular regard to its outcome or effect.[192]

Amazingly, the words just noted to express the miraculous work of Christ and the apostles are also the vocabulary used to describe "the miracles performed in the tribulation by those in allegiance with

Satan."[193] "Signs" is used of satanic miracles in the tribulation (Rev. 13:13–14; 16:14) "and the same combination of words is used: great signs and wonders (Matt. 24:24; Mark 13:22), all power and signs and wonder (2 Thess. 2:9)."[194] Of special note is 2 Thessalonians 2:9, which says of the man of lawlessness that he is "the one whose coming is in accord with the activity of Satan, with all power and signs and false wonders." It sounds like the Bible says there will be miracles, similar to the ones done by our Lord. "The word *pseudos* ('false') has to do with the results of the miracles, not with their lack of genuineness or supernatural origin."[195] The language used by the inspired New Testament writers will not allow for a meaning that these satanic works are just sleight of hand magic tricks, as we shortly shall see.

> **And then that lawless one will be revealed whom the Lord will slay with the breath of His mouth and bring to an end by the appearance of His coming; that is, the one whose coming is in accord with the activity of Satan, with all power and signs and false wonders, and with all the deception of wickedness for those who perish, because they did not receive the love of the truth so as to be saved. And for this reason God will send upon them a deluding influence so that they might believe what is false, in order that they all may be judged who did not believe the truth, but took pleasure in wickedness (2 Thessalonians 2:8–12).**

At times, exactly the same language is used to describe the miracles of Antichrist and the miracles of Jesus and His disciples. This fact supports the notion found in the novels of Tim LaHaye and Jerry Jenkins that the tribulation is a unique time in history in which God permits Satan to do miracles as an evildoer to deceive those who are rejecting Christ's salvation.

## Identical Language

Revelation 13 has much to do with the Beast (also known as the Antichrist) and the False Prophet. The Beast has a "fatal wound [that] was healed" (verse 3), and the False Prophet "makes the earth and those who dwell in it to worship the first Beast, whose fatal wound was healed" (verse 12); "performs great signs, so that he even makes fire come down out of heaven to the earth in the presence of men"[196] (verse 13); "he deceives those who dwell on the earth because of the signs which it was given him to perform in the presence of the Beast, telling those who dwell on the earth to make an image to the Beast who had the wound of the sword and has come to life" (verse 14); and "there was given to him to give breath to the image of the Beast, that the image of the Beast might even speak" (verse 15).

The Greek phrase used in verses 3 and 12 describes the fatal wound to the Beast. John Walvoord, a well-known dispensationalist, suggests this meaning:

> **Another plausible explanation is that the final world ruler receives a wound which normally would be fatal but is miraculously healed by Satan. While the resurrection of a dead person seems to be beyond Satan's power, the healing of a wound would be possible for Satan, and this may be the explanation. The important point is that the final world ruler comes into power obviously supported by a supernatural and miraculous deliverance by Satan himself.[197]**

Walvoord's explanation does not do justice to the language in the passages. We believe that the text supports the actual death and resurrection of the Beast. This is also the view taken by LaHaye and Jenkins in their novel. Gregory Harris explains: "In support of the view that this wound was fatal is the fact that identical language is used of Christ's death and resurrection. Revelation 5:6 describes the Lamb 'as if slain [*hos esphagmenen*]' the same words used of the wound received by the Beast (*hos esphagmenen*, 13:3)."[198] Because of this close similarity Charles Ryrie concludes, "If Christ died actually, then it appears that this ruler will also actually die. But his wound would be healed, which can only mean restoration to life."[199] Non-futurist, Leon Morris also believes that the clearness of the language is too high a hurdle for a non-literal interpreter to navigate and says:

> John's interest is not in how the wound came to be inflicted but in the fact that a wound which appeared to be mortal was healed. He does not tell us how it was healed. He concentrates his attention on the fact that it was healed. Two points only receive emphasis: the deadliness of the wound (*wounded unto death,* and then *his deadly wound*) and the fact of recovery. The expression rendered '*as if . . . wounded*' . . . was used of the Lamb in 5:6, and as the recovery of the Beast is clear there may possibly be the thought of death followed by resurrection. This is one of several places in which the evil one is pictured as parodying Christianity.[200]

Furthermore, "the word referring to the Beast's return to life is similar to the word used of Christ's return to life. Jesus is the One 'who was dead and has come to life [*ezesen*]' (2:8). And the Beast will be the one 'who had the wound of the sword and has come to life [*ezesen*]' (13:14)"[201]

Revelation 17:8, 11 refers to the Beast which "was and is not." Harris notes,

This may well refer to the wounding of the Antichrist in 13:3, 12, and 14. The words "is not" refer to the physical death of the Beast, followed by his ascent from the abyss (17:8), which refers to his return to life (13:14) and is the same as his reappearance as the eighth king of 17:11 .... The twofold reference to the Beast going to destruction or perdition (17:8, 11) is the same as his eternal confinement in the lake of fire (19:20). The description of the Beast in Revelation 17 likewise contains many similarities to the sword-wounded Beast who was healed.[202]

Commentator William Lee concludes: "The language is quite similar, the astonishment of the world's inhabitants identical, and the threefold emphasis on this spectacular feature is repeated in both contexts (13:3, 12, 14; 17:8 bis, 11)."[203]

## Scripture or One's Assumptions

Hanegraaff says the following in his criticism of LaHaye: "In a Christian worldview, only God has the power to raise the dead. If Antichrist could 'raise [himself] from the dead' and control 'the earth and sky,' Christianity would lose the basis for believing that Christ's resurrection vindicates His claim to deity."[204] However, as dispensational commentator Robert Thomas notes, this is "a theological assumption, not an exegetical observation."[205] How can one legitimately conclude *a priori*, as Hanegraaff has done, that something taught in Scripture goes against a Christian worldview? The issue should be: What does the Bible say? Only after Scripture has taught us should we then formulate a Christian worldview. Theological assumptions should not precede exegesis of the Bible. If that approach is used, then one could declare almost anything to be part of a proper Christian worldview and use such an assumption to argue against the actual teaching of the Bible. We believe that this is what Hanegraaff has done in this instance.

Those of us who agree with LaHaye's understanding of these matters do not necessarily believe that Satan is the source of these miraculous events. In fact, we do not. Second Thessalonians 2:11–12 says, "And for this reason God will send upon them a deluding influence so that they might believe what is false, in order that they all may be judged who did not believe the truth, but took pleasure in wickedness." God is the One who enables Satan and his disciples to do these things in a similar way in which He would use any human instrument to work genuine miracles. Harris tells us,

> **The possibility of the Beast's return to life (with either God's sovereign permission or His active working) should not be readily ruled out. In other words, it is not impossible that the Antichrist should return to life because of the unique status of the tribulation and the increased capacity of satanic power during that time,**

as well as God's broadening the parameters of what He will either permit or accomplish directly.[206]

## Historical Beliefs

In Hanegraaff's criticism of LaHaye, he appears to think that only a few extremist futurists, such as LaHaye, would believe that the Beast will be killed and come back to life. Actually, this view has had more advocates than some might realize. We are not saying that the views people have taken on passages of the Bible make it right, but only that some significant figures in church history have held a view similar to LaHaye.

It's interesting to note that even Augustine held a similar view to LaHaye's on this matter (*The City of God*, Book XX, Chapter 19). Another ancient whose views agree with LaHaye's is Lactantius (ca. AD 300) (*Divine Institutes*, Book VII, Chapter 17; *Commentary on the Apocalypse*, Chapter 13). More recent individuals who hold this view include: Lewis Sperry Chafer, J. A. Seiss, Charles C. Ryrie, Leon Morris, Walter K. Price, Robert Govett, and Robert Thomas.[207] LaHaye's view on this matter is not as far-fetched and extreme as Hanegraaff alleges. We support LaHaye on this issue because we, like LaHaye, believe that this is what the Bible teaches.

## CHAPTER SIX

# WHO ARE THE 144,000 JEWS?

⊷ ⊱⊰ ⊶

For the last fifteen years or so when I (Thomas) have heard Hank Hanegraaff, host of the *Bible Answer Man* radio program, field questions on eschatology (end times Bible prophecy), it has become clear that he is decidedly against the futurist perspective. Hanegraaff has told his audience for years that he was studying the field of eschatology and would announce his views in a book one day. Now with the release of *The Apocalypse Code,* he has confirmed the rhetoric and tone I have heard for the last fifteen years on the radio as Hanegraaff has been consistently negative toward dispensationalism. Even though he has insisted that he was open and had not adopted a specific view of eschatology, it has been equally clear to anyone who is schooled in the various views of eschatology that he has all along rejected dispensationalism and embraced his own version of a preterist/idealist scheme. Yet, he has never admitted this. Even after the release of his book, he still refuses to classify his own conclusions in spite of the fact that he assigns labels and outcomes to so many other people's theology.

## Darwin and Darby?

On a number of occasions throughout *AC* Hanegraaff compares LaHaye and dispensationalists to people who are obviously on the shady side of history. The great majority of the book is a broadside against Hanegraaff's distorted view of dispensationalism in general and LaHaye in particular. An example of this occurs when Hanegraaff weaves an extended comparison between John Nelson Darby, the formulator of modern dispensationalism, and Charles Darwin, an influential spokesman for evolution. In one chapter he spends the first twelve pages developing a Darwin/Darby comparison and then brings up his wild parallel at the close of the chapter.[208] In the process of describing Darwin's influence upon others, Hanegraaff lists such ungodly individuals as Hitler, Karl Marx, Sigmund Freud, and Margaret Sanger. Why? Apparently Hanegraaff prefaces his discussion of Darby with the Darwin and friends section in an attempt to prejudice his readers against Darby. Hanegraaff says, "In 1831—the same year that Charles Darwin left England and sailed into evolutionary infamy aboard the HMS *Beagle*—another nineteenth-century dogma with profound consequences for the history of humanity was birthed in the British Isles."[209] He then proceeds to talk about Darby:

Like Darwin, however, Darby was a trendsetter. In much the same way that Darwin imposed a speculative spin on the scientific data he encountered along the South American coasts of Patagonia, Darby imposed a subjective spin on the scriptural data he encountered in the city of Plymouth.[210]

This is a reckless comparison that is generally untrue. Darby and the Brethren of his day were largely of a traditional orthodoxy concerning an overwhelming

116

majority of their doctrine. Darby did not really press his views of Bible prophecy until the mid-1840s,[211] even though he had clearly developed his view of the pre-trib rapture by 1833, and most likely before that time. Further, Hanegraaff says, "Darby imposed a subjective spin on the scriptural data he encountered in the city of Plymouth," as if Darby was from Plymouth, England, or resided there. The Brethren were often called "Plymouth Brethren" since the largest, early assembly was in Plymouth, England. Darby was from Ireland and first started meeting with the Brethren there, not in England. Darby did visit the church in Plymouth a few times, but only spent a couple of months there.[212] It is unlikely that he developed or "spun" any of his theology in Plymouth since he spent such little time there. No wonder Norman Geisler says, "There is a wild comparison of John Nelson Darby's dispensationalism with Darwin's evolutionary dogma. Other than the time period in which they wrote there is very little agreement between the two."[213] Interestingly, Darby describes himself as, "a conservative by birth, by education and by mind."[214] Darby is hardly one who would have been of the liberal mindset to have anything in common with Darwin.

## Plan B?

Throughout this book Hanegraaff also often misrepresents the views of dispensationalism and creates what Geisler has described as a straw man attack.[215] Hanegraaff says, "Contrary to popularists such as LaHaye, the new covenant is not a mere 'plan B' that God instituted as a parenthesis between two phases of His redemptive work with Israel."[216]

Dispensationalists do not believe that God has a plan B in any way, shape, or form. In almost thirty-five years, since I have become a dispensationalist, I (Thomas) have never heard or read of a dispensationalist teaching the plan B scenario. Hanegraaff appears to want to cast LaHaye in a bad light. (Notice no footnote by Hanegraaff to document his allegation.) Yet opponents often present this straw man in their statements of what we supposedly believe in order to make us look incoherent or to make it appear that we think God failed and must try again with a plan B for history. Nonsense! We believe that God's single plan has always included the church, but He did not reveal the Church Age part of the plan in the Old Testament. This is the teaching of Paul in Romans 16:25–27; Ephesians 2 and 3; and Colossians 1 and 2 in which he says that this truth is a mystery, never before revealed in the Old Testament.

Paul states specifically in Ephesians that the Church Age "was in accordance with the eternal purpose which He carried out in Christ Jesus our Lord" (3:11). This is why dispensationalists have never taught the so-called plan A and plan B theory that critics suppose we hold. Dispensationalists have always taught that there is a single plan carried out in stages. Those things which relate to Israel were previously revealed, while those things relating to the church were hidden until after the birth of Christ's body. Verse 8 says it is "the manifold wisdom of God," meaning many-sided wisdom of God. Non-dispensational scholar, Ernest Best, commenting on Ephesians 3:5 said: "There is both continuity and discontinuity between the testaments: our passage stressed the discontinuity."[217] Thus, God's single plan has multiple aspects (dispensations) to it. Both unity and diversity is a part of God's plan. Dispensationalists recognize both God's single plan and that it is worked out in history progressively through various stages, while many like Hanegraaff too often deny genuine biblical distinctions by following allegorical interpretative approaches like his $e^2$.

## Another Bad Comparison

In *AC*, Hanegraaff introduces a section on the 144,000 Jews from Revelation 7 and 14 by juxtaposing the Jehovah's Witnesses cult with Tim LaHaye. "Like Watchtower founder Charles Taze Russell, Tim LaHaye believes that God has two distinct people with two distinct plans and two distinct destinies," claims Hanegraaff. "Unlike the Watchtower, however, he holds that the 144,000 are Jewish witnesses, not Jehovah's Witnesses. There is not a Gentile among them. Nor for that matter are there any women."[218] As president of the Christian Research Institute, a counter-cult ministry, Hanegraaff's comparison is especially cryptic and extremely misguided to characterize an orthodox Christian brother like LaHaye in such a derogatory manner. Yet, he makes these kinds of comparisons throughout his book.[219]

As is so often the case in *AC*, Hanegraaff's comparative illustration contains mistakes and error. The Watchtower and Jehovah Witness cult does not teach "that God has two distinct people with two distinct plans and two distinct destinies," as characterized by Hanegraaff.[220]

## Who are the 144,000?

Hanegraaff says that his interpretive approach leads him to understand that the 144,000 of Revelation 7 and 14 is "the purified bride," or "true Israel," which is the church.[221] This is a classic replacement theology interpretation whether Hanegraaff realizes it or not. He then continues to torture the biblical text by equating the 144,000 from every tribe of the sons of Israel (Rev. 7:4) with another group of believers said by the biblical text to be "a great multitude, which no one can count from every nation and all tribes and peoples and tongues" (Rev. 7:9). He says, "The 144,000 and the great multitude are not two different peoples, but two different ways of describing the same purified bride."[222] So what does the Bible actually teach? The Bible teaches what the text says, not what Hanegraaff imagines and imposes upon the text via his allegorical alchemy, which he masquerades as exegetical eschatology.

Here is why this passage means what it says and refers to exactly 144,000 Jewish guys (no gals or Gentiles included), and 12,000 from each of the twelve tribes of Israel. First, at this point in Revelation John is writing down what he hears the angel who is crying out with a loud voice say (Rev. 7:2, 4). The angel says they are a specific number of Jewish men.

Second, if this was some kind of code word or metaphor for something else then there should be an indication in the context that such is the case. However, there is no such textual indication. Hanegraaff clearly rejects the plain meaning of the passage: "And I heard the number of those who were sealed, one hundred and forty-four thousand sealed from every tribe of the sons of Israel" (Rev. 7:4). Dallas Seminary professor, Roy Zuck (a dispensationalist) has written an excellent book on how to interpret the Bible.[223] In a chapter dealing with figures of speech, Zuck says, "Generally an expression is figurative when it is out of character with the subject discussed, or is contrary to fact, experience, or observation."[224] Dispensationalist E. W. Bullinger has written what is probably the most comprehensive book ever called *Figures of Speech Used in the Bible: Explained and Illustrated*.[225] "E. W. Bullinger grouped the Bible's figures of speech into more than 200 categories, giving 8,000 illustrations from the Scriptures," [226] notes Zuck. Bullinger defines a figure of speech as "simply a word or a sentence thrown into a peculiar form, different from its original or simplest meaning or use."[227] Zuck provides six guidelines to aid one in determining whether a word or phrase is figurative. Some of the most helpful include:

**(1) Always take a passage in its literal sense unless there is good reason for doing otherwise. (2) The figurative sense is intended if the literal would involve an impossibility. (3) The figurative is intended if the literal meaning is an absurdity."[228]**

Pastor Matthew Waymeyer agrees and provides the following simple formula: "In order to be considered symbolic, the language in question must possess (a) some degree of *absurdity* when taken literally and (b) some degree of *clarity* when taken symbolically.[229]

Third, Hanegraaff attempts to support his allegorical interpretation[230] that the 144,000 is the "purified bride" or the "true Israel" by saying "the pattern of Scripture is to refer to the community of faith, whether Jew or Gentile, with Jewish designations."[231] No, that is simply not true! He fails to provide one valid example to back up his erroneous claim. In his lone attempt to support his view Hanegraaff says, "New Jerusalem itself is figuratively built on the foundation of the twelve apostles and is entered through twelve gates inscribed with the names of the twelve tribes of Israel. Not only so, but its walls are twelve times twelve, or 144, cubits thick (Revelation 21:12–17)."[232] This statement provides no proof of his contention. The New Jerusalem refers to the eternal state where Jewish and Gentile believers will dwell together in a single city, the New Jerusalem. Why doesn't the passage denote Jewish believers in its reference to the twelve tribes of Israel, while the twelve apostles indicate Gentile believers?[233] His "proof" of this pattern demonstrates the opposite. As Robert Thomas notes, "A tie-in of the term to the church through the twelve apostles (cf. Matt. 19:28) is improbable because Rev. 21:12, 14 makes a clear distinction between the two groups of twelve."[234] If it was truly the pattern of Scripture to use Jewish designations for the community of faith, whether Jew or Gentile, then Hanegraaff should have been able to provide more than his single example that is questionable. Instead the pattern of Scripture is just the opposite.

There is not a single passage in the entire New Testament where language that speaks of Israel or the Jews ever is used to refer to anyone who is not ethnically

Israel. Hebrew Christian Arnold Fruchtenbaum, in his Ph.D. dissertation,[235] has studied every use of Israel in the New Testament[236] and says, "The conclusion is that the church is never called, and is not, a 'spiritual Israel' or a 'new Israel.' The term *Israel* is either used of the nation or the people as a whole, or of the believing remnant within. It is never used of the church in general or of Gentile believers in particular."[237] Thomas says, "No clear cut example of the church being called 'Israel' exists in the NT or in ancient church writings until AD 160."[238] So it was well after the close of the canon of Scripture, after the apostolic era that such a view was even first suggested. Therefore, this argument cannot be a basis for taking a non-literal interpretation of the 144,000.

Fourth, Hanegraaff believes that the numbers in this passage are symbolic and do not represent their stated value. To begin with, it is important to realize that any counting number (i.e., one, two, three, etc.) is in fact a symbol for the number of items that it references, in this case 144,000 "sons of Israel." His interpretation of the 144,000 is a case in point. Bible scholar Nathaniel West punned about 125 years ago, for those like Hanegraaff, "symbolical numbers don't count."[239] Geisler observes that Hanegraaff "is so mesmerized by symbols that he even has symbols of symbols."[240] So it is in this instance, Hanegraaff's idealism generated by his own imagination, ungoverned by Scripture, imagines that these numbers don't count. He says, "To suggest as LaHaye does that '12,000' from each of the twelve tribes means exactly 12,000—not 11,999 or 12,001—must surely stretch the credulity of even the most ardent literalist beyond the breaking point."[241] In spite of such rhetoric, he does not believe that numbers count in this instance. Why would it be silly, as he appears to think, that God would chose exactly 144,000 sons of Israel or 12,000 from each of the twelve tribes of Israel? How does that stretch the credulity of those of us who think that is what God meant by what He said? Does he think that God cannot count that high? That God is only good with small numbers but becomes sloppy and imprecise if He uses large numbers? The Lord could have said, "12,000 from each tribe in Israel, give or take a few."

The use of 144,000 and 12,000 twelve times is not a valid reason to say that these numbers don't count. "The prophecy of the 144,000 in 7:4–8 need not be considered a symbolic number," insists Zuck. "The number is to be taken in its normal, literal sense because 12,000 people are said to be sealed from each of the twelve tribes of Israel. Since the tribal names are literal and not symbolic, there is no reason to take the numbers symbolically."[242] In absence of a textual reason by Hanegraaff to take the numbers non-literally and since they make good sense if you do take them literally, they should be taken as literal numbers that refer to a future group of Jewish men.

Fifth, the 144,000 are painstakingly broken down into a division of 12,000 each. The text says, " . . . from every tribe of the sons of Israel" (Rev. 7:4). Then Scripture goes on to repeat the same language twelve times, " . . . from the tribe of Judah, twelve thousand were sealed, from the tribe of Reuben twelve thousand, from the tribe of Gad twelve thousand" (Rev. 7:5) and so on to include the twelve tribes of Israel (Rev. 7:5–8). Verse 8 ends by saying, " . . . from the tribe of Benjamin, twelve thousand were sealed." How does any of this support a figurative interpretation? How is this language figurative and what in the text supports such a notion? Every one of the tribal names is literal and not symbolic. Thomas concludes:

**Israel has not and will not lose her distinctive national identity before God, regardless of human proposal to the contrary. Hence support for a literal understanding of the proper names in this paragraph is the outgrowth of interpreting the Bible in its natural sense. Any other interpretation has to struggle for supporting evidence.**[243]

Sixth, Hanegraaff makes his strangest claim thus far when he attempts to support his allegorical view as follows: "Ten of the twelve tribes lost their national identity almost three thousand years ago in the Assyrian exile. The other two, Judah and Benjamin, were largely decimated two thousand years ago by Roman hordes."[244] The obvious answer to this notion is a biblical view of God. Even though the identity of the tribe members may be lost to mankind, "it is still known to God who will be in charge of sealing when it takes place, so this view is not prohibitive to the literal view."[245]

Scholar Jeffrey Louie provides further answers to Hanegraaff's argument in his Ph.D. dissertation on the 144,000. Louie notes that such a view as Hanegraaff advances "can only be described as a presumption based upon ignorance. The concept of a total deportation is not a viable position."[246] Louie notes from 2 Chronicles 30 that many from the northern kingdom came down to the southern kingdom and were preserved. Even though a majority from the northern kingdom was taken into captivity by the Assyrians, many from the ten tribes remained in the land of Israel. Louie also documents that those taken into captivity maintained their identity while outside the land.[247] Louie further documents that "the Ashkenazim are mainly the descendants of Judah and Benjamin, and the Sepharadim and Oriental Jews are mainly the descendants of the ten northern tribes." Louie describes the position of Hanegraaff as "weak" and then concludes: "Although the tribal genealogies no longer exist, it is wrong to conclude that the descendants of the northern tribes also no longer exist. The northern heritage exists in the modern Jewish population."[248]

Those who agree with Hanegraaff on this issue also forget that only sixty years after the destruction of Jerusalem in AD 70, the Jews staged a second revolt against the Romans led by Bar Kokhba. If the Jews had lost their identity after AD 70, then how were they able to revolt against Rome in AD 132? At this time they retook Jerusalem, built a makeshift temple, as depicted by coins from the time, and declared their leader to be their messiah. The Roman Emperor Hadrian came and put down this revolt and killed about half a million Jews in AD 135. How could this have happened if the Jews had lost their identity before this time? Too bad the Muslims and Christians of the Middle Ages did not know that Jews had lost their identity in the first century AD. There would have been millions who would not have been tortured, raped, and killed. If only Hitler had known that the Jews were not really descendants of Abraham, Isaac, and Jacob.

Seventh, as already noted, Hanegraaff equates the 144,000 with the passage that follows in verse 9, saying, "the 144,000 are *a great multitude* that no one could count, from every nation, tribe, people and language, standing before the throne and in front of the Lamb.'"[249] He tells us that contrary to LaHaye's understanding, "the 144,000 and the great multitude are not two different peoples, but two different ways of describing the same purified bride."[250] Once again, one could not come up with such a view from reading the biblical text. Extra-textual ideas must be imported into the passage. Verse 9 begins with the prepositional phrase, "After these things," (which Hanegraaff omits from his quotation of the passage). After what things? After the sealing of the 144,000 *on earth* the scene turns *to heaven* and a totally different group of people and events. "This group, like the 144,000, is unhurt by the effects of God's wrath, but for a different reason," notes Thomas. "They have at this point been removed from the earthly scene of the wrath and have no need of protective sealing."[251]

Nothing in the context supports Hanegraaff's idea that the 144,000 and the great multitude are one and the same. (1) The 144,000 were carefully numbered as twelve groups of 12,000, while the second group is innumerable, "which no one could count." How could it be that a precise number is given to the group of Jewish men, while the second group is said to be so vast that it would be impossible for humans to count them, if they are supposed to be the same group? (2) The first group was said to be Jews "from every tribe of the sons of Israel," while the second group is said to be from "every nation and all tribes and peoples and tongues." (3) The 144,000 are sealed in order to protect them from the impending trumpet judgments about to befall planet Earth, while the great multitude has been delivered from the impending wrath through martyrdom and are safely in heaven. "This multitude includes far more than the 144,000 of the earlier group."[252]

If these are two different groups, then an interesting and exciting relationship is implied between them. Israel's calling is to be a light to the nations. She has thus far not done a very good job. However, in the tribulation she will make progress toward becoming that light she was set apart to be. The 144,000 Jewish men will be like having thousands of apostle Pauls out evangelizing the nations. The result will be millions of conversions to Christ among the Gentiles, even though many will have to give their lives as described in verse 9. The 144,000 Jews, like Paul, are supernaturally converted at some point after the rapture of the church. Since the rapture leaves believers without mature leadership, the supernatural protection of God's seal will enable the 144,000 to become fearless preachers of the gospel during such a physically demanding time. This cause/effect view that we have just given better explains this passage than Hanegraaff's both/and view.

## Conclusion

Rather than helping the student of the Bible better understand what it says concerning the 144,000 and other prophetic issues, Hanegraaff's interpretive approach clouds and obfuscates the intended meaning of the text. Furthermore, in the process of applying his approach, not only does he not discover the true meaning of the Bible on these matters, he too often manufactures issues which he uses to attack those with whom he disagrees. Hanegraaff needs to adopt the tried and true historical-grammatical hermeneutic so that he will not stray so far from the plain meaning of God's prophetic Word. If he were more in touch hermeneutically with the reality of biblical prophecy teachings then it would reduce his desire to attack more orthodox teachers like Tim LaHaye.

## CHAPTER seven

# WHAT ABOUT MODERN ISRAEL?

⊷ ⊨✦⊨ ⊶

In *AC*, Hanegraaff teaches that national Israel has been permanently replaced by the church and does not have a prophetic future as a nation. "All of the types and shadows of the old covenant, including the holy land of Israel, the holy city Jerusalem, and the holy temple of God," claims Hanegraaff, "have been fulfilled in the Holy Christ."[253] We agree with one aspect of what he says that Christ has fulfilled all the types and shadows of the old covenant. However, Hanegraaff is wrong to include unfulfilled promises and prophecy as mere types and shadows. Promises related to Israel and Jerusalem are based upon prophecy that has not yet been fulfilled, thus, not a mere type or shadow. Historically, the theology of those who believe that national Israel does not have a future is called "replacement theology" or "supersessionism." (This word is used for those who believe that the church has *superseded* Israel.)

## What about Replacement Theology?
Replacement theology "is the view that the church is the new or true Israel that has permanently replaced or superseded Israel as the people of God."[254] Another term,

often found in academic circles, for replacement theology is the older term supersessionism.[255] Replacement theology has been the fuel within Christendom that has energized medieval anti-Semitism, Eastern European pogroms, the Holocaust, and contemporary disdain for the modern state of Israel. Masters Seminary professor Mike Vlach notes: "The acceptance or rejection of supersessionism may also influence how one views the modern state of Israel and events in the Middle East."[256] Wherever replacement theology has flourished, the Jews have had to run for cover.

In a response to a review of *AC*, Hanegraaff said, "I have never argued for replacement theology."[257] This is a surprising statement since his book is filled with replacement theological statements and arguments. This provides further support that Hanegraaff regularly avoids classification of his theological conclusions. He gives the following reason for denying that he holds supersessionist views:

> **God has only ever had one chosen people who form one covenant community, beautifully symbolized in Scripture by one cultivated olive tree. Indeed, the precise terminology used to describe the children of Israel in the Old Testament is ascribed to the church in the New Testament .... As such, the true church is true Israel, and true Israel is truly the church—one cannot replace what it already is. Rather than reason together in collegial debate, dispensationalists have coined the phrase "replacement theologian" as the ultimate silencer.[258]**

Hanegraaff errs in thinking that replacement theology was invented by dispensationalists to name-call those who disagree with them. "While it is true that Israel occupies an important place in dispensational theology, it is also true that reflection concerning the place of Israel in God's plan predates this school of thought by many centuries,"[259] notes scholar Ronald Diprose. While an early form of replacement theology began in the second century with Justin Martyr, Diprose describes it as consisting of the belief that "Israel has been repudiated by God and has been replaced by the church in the working out of His plan. A variation of this idea is that true Israel always has been the church,"[260] which is the view expressed by Hanegraaff throughout *AC*.[261]

Mike Vlach, in his Ph.D. dissertation on the subject, describes both the method of replacement theology and the theology or outcome it produces:

> **In the realm of hermeneutics, supersessionists argue that: (1) the New Testament has interpretive priority over the Old Testament; (2) national Israel functioned as a type of the New Testament church; and (3) the New Testament indicates that Old Testament prophecies regarding national Israel are being fulfilled with the church.**[262]

It is obvious when reading *AC* that Hanegraaff has adopted the hermeneutics or method of replacement theology.

That the New Testament has interpretive priority over the Old is seen throughout *AC* as Hanegraaff dismisses Old Testament prophecy that has never been fulfilled for Israel by subsuming it into a supposed New Testament fulfillment. For example, by characterizing Israel in the Old Testament as "the prostituted bride" who is replaced in the New Testament by "the purified bride," which is the church, Hanegraaff reinterprets the Old in light of the New.[263] After comparing a number of Old Testament characters with Jesus of the New Testament (for example, Joshua and Jesus), Hanegraaff says, "In each case, the lesser is fulfilled and rendered obsolete by the greater."[264] We agree that the New Testament often mentions God's progress in revelation by noting Christ's fulfillment of the Old, but nowhere does the New indicate that Old Testament promises to ethnic Israel are superseded by Christ's work. Instead, Christ is the basis for the fulfillment of Old Testament promises. Hanegraaff says, the "old covenant shadows find their final consummation in the person and work of Jesus Christ."[265] It is not an either/or situation as Hanegraaff puts forth; it is best to see the relationship between the testaments as a both/and.

Vlach's second methodological point is that advocates of replacement theology see national Israel as a type of the New Testament church. Such an approach is clearly advocated throughout *AC*, especially in the chapter on the typology principle, which is his longest chapter. "Jerusalem symbolized all that Israel was to be .... Jerusalem is typological of the greater purposes of God,"[266] declares Hanegraaff. He speaks of Paul illustrating a "typologically heightened fulfillment ... that all who fixate on an earthly Jerusalem with a rebuilt temple and reinstituted temple sacrifices are in slavery to types and shadows."[267] Hanegraaff speaks of "the typological fulfillment of the temple and the rest of the old covenant."[268] His views on this matter are clearly stated throughout *AC* and are summarized as follows: "The New Testament's typological interpretation of the Old Testament thus stands as the ultimate corrective to Zionist zeal."[269]

The third point, that the Old Testament promises to Israel are fulfilled with the church is also evident within *AC*. Hanegraaff says, "the land promises are fully and finally fulfilled in the final future through Jesus . . . the promise is typologically fulfilled in the Lord."[270] Again he says, "Peter uses the very language once reserved for national Israel and applies it to spiritual Israel."[271] "Furthermore, the land promises are fulfilled in the far future through Jesus who provides true Israel with permanent rest from their wanderings in sin."[272] Hanegraaff uses the term "true Israel" as a reference to the church.[273]

Vlach also describes the theological arguments that supersessionists construct:

> **(1) the New Testament teaches the permanent rejection of national Israel as the people of God; (2) application of "Israel" language to the church shows that the church is now the true Israel; (3) salvific unity between Jews and Gentiles rules out a restoration of national Israel; and (4) fulfillment of the new covenant with the church shows that the church is now the true Israel.**[274]

There is no doubt that Hanegraaff holds to these theological outcomes as a result of his interpretive approach.

In fact, Hanegraaff even uses the term "superseded" in the following replacement theology statement: "History, like the New Testament, reveals that the Holy City—turned harlot city—is superseded by the holy Christ. Jesus is the antitype who fulfills all of the typology vested in Jerusalem."[275] Hanegraaff says that Genesis 12:3, which we take to include ethnic Israel, refers instead "to true Israel, which consists of every person who through faith has been adopted into the family of God."[276] When speaking of the land promises which have never yet been completely fulfilled, he insists that they are "fulfilled and rendered obsolete by the greater."[277] Such is a classic replacement theology statement. Hanegraaff quotes approvingly from fellow supersessionist Stephen Sizer who says, "The purpose of the temple, therefore, finds its ultimate significance and fulfillment not in another man-made sanctuary but in Jesus Christ and His church."[278]

We may safely conclude that in spite of his denials, Hanegraaff is clearly an advocate of replacement theology. Norm Geisler also understands that *AC* teaches replacement theology when he notes, "In general *The Code* repeatedly takes the Old Testament promises to Jews out of their original context by replacing Israel with the New Testament church. The 'replacement theology' is a classic example of taking texts out of their context."[279] Even though Hanegraaff believes that God is finished with Israel, what does the Bible really teach on this matter?

## Modern Israel's Right to The Land

All throughout the Old Testament God says that the land we know as Israel is for the descendants of Abraham, Isaac and Jacob, or the Jews. Every Old Testament prophet, except Jonah, speaks of a permanent return to the land of Israel by the Jews.[280] Nowhere in the New Testament are these Old Testament promises ever changed or negated.[281] In fact, they are reinforced by some New Testament passages (Matt. 19:28; Acts 1:6). Old Testament scholar Walter Kaiser notes that "the writer of Hebrews (6:13, 17–18) . . . swore by Himself when He made the promise: to show how immutable His purpose was."[282] Paul declares of the promises to Israel: "for the gifts and the calling of God are irrevocable" (Rom. 11:29).

The only legitimate basis for the Jews to claim a right to the land of Israel comes from God and the Bible. In fact, if it were not for the biblical history of Israel, who would even know to associate the Jewish people with the land of Israel? It is precisely because God associates the Jewish people with the land that He gave them—located in today's Middle East—that we could even have a movement today known as Zionism. Detractors of Zionism, like Hanegraaff, must attempt to say that God's promise of the land of Israel to the Jews has somehow been invalidated. Many have tried down through the years to prove just that! But God's Word speaks louder than their shrill voices combined.

Hanegraaff insists that he is not opposed to the modern state of Israel. All we found was a lone statement in *AC* that said, "The modern state of Israel has a definitive right to exist."[283] However, when compared to his constant and regular criticism of Israel as one who is alleged to oppress the Palestinians, it hardly seems sincere. He provides no support for Israel beyond that statement. The case for Zionism rises or falls upon what the Bible teaches about Israel and the land of Israel. It is true that a just case for Israel can be presented upon many grounds, but ultimately it boils down to what God thinks about this matter as communicated through His inerrant and authoritative Word—the Bible.

## God's Promise of the Land

The Lord called Abram out of Ur of the Chaldeans and made an unconditional covenant, or contract, with him. This contract, known as the Abrahamic covenant, contains three major elements: (1) a land to Abram and his descendants, Israel, (2) a seed or physical descendants of Abraham, and (3) a worldwide blessing (Gen. 12:1–3). Hanegraaff says, "Christian Zionists are convinced that these promises God made to Abraham, Isaac, and Jacob with respect to the land are unconditional and yet unfulfilled."[284] Yes, we do and here is why!

In order to make it clear that this promise was to be an unconditional covenant, the Lord put Abram to sleep and made Himself the only signatory of the contract (Gen. 15:1–21). God told Abram, "To your descendants I have given this land" (verse 18). Even though the Lord was the only active signatory to the cutting of the covenant, nevertheless it is clear that Abraham obeyed the Lord during his lifetime. The Lord declared: "Abraham obeyed Me and kept My charge, My commandments, My statutes and My laws" (Gen. 26:5). John Walvoord observes, "It is significant that the promise is related to Abraham's obedience, not to Isaac's, as the promise now becomes immutable and certain of fulfillment."[285] This covenant is repeated to Abraham, Isaac, and Jacob and their descendants about twenty times in the book of Genesis.[286] God's promise to the patriarchs is said to be an everlasting covenant (Gen. 17:7, 13, 19).

The promise of the land covenant is passed from Abraham to Isaac, instead of Ishmael. The Lord told Isaac:

> Sojourn in this land and I will be with you and bless you, for to you and to your descendants I will give all these lands, and I will establish the oath which I swore to your father Abraham. And I will multiply your descendants as the stars of heaven, and will give your descendants all these lands; and by your descendants all the nations of the earth shall be blessed (Gen. 26:3–4).

Here we see a duplication of God's promise to Isaac's father (cf. Gen. 12:3; 15:18).

Number three in the patriarchal descent is Jacob, rather than Esau. Jacob's name is later changed to Israel, which becomes the primary name of the new nation. In Jacob's famous dream of a stairway from heaven to earth, the Lord said,

> I am the Lord, the God of your father Abraham and the God of Isaac; the land on which you lie, I will give it to you and to your descendants. Your descendants shall also be like the dust of the earth, and you shall spread out to the west and to the east and to the north and to the south; and in you and in your descendants shall all the families of the earth be blessed" (Gen. 28:13–14).

This statement also includes a repetition of the land promise made to Abraham and Isaac and would be passed on to Jacob's posterity, fulfilled in his twelve sons, the twelve tribes of Israel, and their descendants. Walvoord notes:

> A careful study of these passages makes clear that the promise of the land was intrinsic to the whole covenant given to Abraham. Inasmuch as Abraham became a great man, had a great posterity, and brought blessing to the whole world through Christ, it is reasonable to assume that the rest of the Abrahamic covenant will be fulfilled just as literally as these provisions. The nonliteral or conditional interpretation of these promises is not supported in Scripture.[287]

Genesis closes with Jacob, his twelve sons and their descendants sojourning in the land of Egypt. Exodus is the story of their deliverance from Egypt and preparation for entrance into the land of Canaan. Even though Israel wandered in the wilderness for forty years because of unbelief, it was there that Moses received the Law that would become the new nation's constitution.

The book of Deuteronomy says at least twenty-five times that the land is a gift to the people of Israel from the Lord (Deut. 1:20, 25; 2:29; 3:20; 4:40; 5:16, etc.). Old Testament scholar Walter Kaiser notes that "sixty-nine times the writer of Deuteronomy repeated the pledge that Israel would one day 'possess' and 'inherit' the land promised to her."[288]

Deuteronomy 28–30 lays out the conditions for Israel to experience blessing within the land.

We must remember that while the land was given unconditionally to the people of Israel, the Mosaic Law provides subconditions for the nation to enjoy God's blessings in the land. The tribulation period will be a time of divine discipline on the nation, bringing about Israel's repentance and obedience. And then, during those grand and golden days of the millennial kingdom, she will experience full occupation of her land, reaping the many blessings promised in the Old Testament.

The Psalms, Israel's handbook of praise to the Lord, often lead the worshiper in thanksgiving to the Lord for His covenant promises and faithfulness. For example, Psalm 105 says, "He has remembered His covenant forever, the word which He commanded to a thousand generations, the covenant which He made with Abraham, and His oath to Isaac. Then He confirmed it to Jacob for a statute, to Israel as an everlasting covenant, saying, 'To you I will give the land of Canaan as the portion of your inheritance'" (Psalm 105:8–11). Elsewhere in the Psalms, the Lord declares: "For the LORD has chosen Zion; He has desired it for His habitation. 'This is My resting place forever; Here I will dwell, for I have desired it'" (Psalm 123:13–14). God's choice of providing the land of Israel for the Jewish people has remained steadfast down through history.

Throughout the Old Testament the prophets convict Israel of her disobedience, but always with a view toward a future restoration, when ultimately Israel will dwell in peace and prosperity. However,

141

Hanegraaff only quotes Old Testament passages that speak of when Israel is in rebellion to the Lord. It is true that the Old Testament often portrays Israel as a great prostitute as the *AC* demonstrates.[289] The problem with Hanegraaff's depiction is that he does not tell his readers all that the Old Testament says about Israel. Instead, he says that the Lord permanently rejects Israel because of her unfaithful ways and replaces her with the bride of Christ, the New Testament church.[290] However, Hanegraaff has withheld from his readers the fact that the Old Testament does not stop with an unfaithful Israel, it tells us the rest of the story.

The Old Testament prophets pick up where Hanegraaff leaves off and provides promise after promise of a time of future restoration to the land (Isa. 11:1–9; 12:1–3; 27:12–13; 35:1–10; 43:1–8; 60:18–21; 66:20–22; Jer. 16:14–16; 30:10–18; 31:31–37; 32:37–40; Ezek. 11:17–21; 28:25–26; 34:11–16; 37:21–25; 39:25–29; Hosea 1:10–11; 3:4–5; Joel 3:17–21; Amos 9:11–15; Micah 4:4–7; Zeph. 3: 14–20; Zech. 8:4–8; 10:11–15). A specific example of a restoration passage can be found at the end of Amos:

> "Also I will restore the captivity of My people Israel, and they will rebuild the ruined cities and live in them, they will also plant vineyards and drink their wine, and make gardens and eat their fruit. I will also plant them on their land, and they will not again be rooted out from their land which I have given them," says the LORD your God (Amos 9:14–15).

It is important to note that Zechariah, following the return from the Babylonian captivity, speaks of a future restoration to the land, thus suggesting that Israel's past restorations did not ultimately fulfill the land promise given to Abraham, Isaac, and Jacob. Zechariah 9–14 lays out an end-time plan of restoration of the nation to Jerusalem and the land of Israel. Kaiser notes:

> **Repeatedly, the prophets of the Old Testament had depicted an Israelite remnant returning to the land (e.g., Isa. 10:20–30) and becoming prominent among the nations (Mic. 4:1) at the end of days. In fact, Zechariah 10:8–12 is still repeating this same promise in 518 BC, well after the days when many in Israel had returned from their last and final exile, the Babylonian exile.[291]**

Further, Israel has a future in their land since nowhere in the Bible has the Lord specifically revoked any of His promises to His people Israel: "for the gifts and the calling of God are irrevocable" (Rom. 11:29).

## Multiple End-Time Regatherings

To properly understand the end-time homecoming or regathering of the Jews to their Promised Land, we need to keep five major points in mind. Let us look briefly at each of these five points and see what the Bible says.

1) The Bible predicts that Israel will experience two worldwide, end-time regatherings to the Promised Land.

Dozens of biblical passages predict these global events. It is a common mistake, however, to lump all of these passages into one fulfillment time frame, especially in relation to the current state of Israel. Modern Israel is prophetically significant and is fulfilling Bible prophecy. But we need to be careful to distinguish which passages are being fulfilled in our day and which await a further future fulfillment.

In short, there will be two end-time regatherings: one before the tribulation and one after the tribulation. The first worldwide regathering will be a return in unbelief, in preparation for the judgment of the tribulation. The second worldwide regathering will be a return in faith at the end of the tribulation, in preparation for the blessing of the millennial reign of Christ.[292]

One important passage that deals with Israel's two regatherings is Isaiah 11:11–12:

> Then it will happen on that day that the Lord will again recover *the second time* with His hand the remnant of His people, who will remain, from Assyria, Egypt, Pathros, Cush, Elam, Shinar, Hamath, and from the islands of the sea. And He will lift up a standard for the nations, and will assemble the banished ones of Israel, and will gather the dispersed of Judah from the four corners of the earth (emphasis added).

The return in Isaiah 11 clearly refers to the final worldwide regathering of Israel in faith, at the climax of the tribulation, and in preparation for the millennial kingdom. Isaiah specifically says that this final regathering is the second one. That, of course, raises the obvious question: When did the first regathering occur?

Some maintain that the first return is the Babylonian return from the exile that began in about 536 BC. But how could this return be described as *worldwide*, as set forth in Isaiah 11?[293]

Arnold Fruchtenbaum writes:

**The entire context is Isaiah 11:11–12:6. In this context, he is speaking of the final worldwide regathering in faith in preparation for blessing. Isaiah numbers the final worldwide regathering in faith in preparation of the messianic kingdom as the *second* one. In other words, the last one is only the second one. If the last one is the second one, how many can there be before that? Only one. The first one could not have been the return from Babylon since that was not an international regathering from the four corners of the world, only a migration from one country (Babylonia) to another (Judea). The Bible does not allow for several worldwide regatherings in unbelief; it allows for *one* worldwide regathering in unbelief; followed by the last one, the one in faith, which is the second one. This text only permits two worldwide regatherings from *the four corners of the earth*. Therefore, the present Jewish state *is* very relevant to Bible prophecy.[294]**

The following chart provides a quick visual comparison and contrast between Israel's two great regatherings.[295]

| THE PRESENT (FIRST) REGATHERING | THE PERMANENT (SECOND) REGATHERING |
|---|---|
| Worldwide | Worldwide |
| Return to part of the land | Return to all the land |
| Return in unbelief | Return in faith |
| Restored to the land only | Restored to the land and the Lord |
| Man's work (secular) | God's work (spiritual) |
| Sets the stage for the tribulation (discipline) | Sets the stage for the millennium (blessing) |

Here are some of the key Scripture passages related to each of these regatherings:

| ISRAEL—Regathered Before the Tribulation in Unbelief (Current State of the Nation) | ISRAEL—Regathered Before the Millennium in Belief (Future State) |
|---|---|
| Ezekiel 20:33–38; 22:17–22; 36:22–24 | Deuteronomy 4:29–31; 30:1–10 |
| Isaiah 11:11–12 | Isaiah 27:12–13; 43:5–7 |
| Zephaniah 2:1–2 | Jeremiah 16:14–15; 31:7–10 |
| Ezekiel 38–39 | Ezekiel 11:14–18 |
| | Amos 9:14–15 |
| | Zechariah 10:8–12 |
| | Matthew 24:31 |

# First Worldwide Gathering in Unbelief

2) The first worldwide regathering, in unbelief, will set the stage for the events of the tribulation period.

When the modern state of Israel was born in 1948, it not only became an important stage-setting development, but also began an actual fulfillment of specific Bible prophecies about an international regathering of the Jews in unbelief before the judgment of the tribulation. The following Old Testament passages predict this development: Ezek. 20:33–38; 22:17–22; 36:22–24; 37:1–14; Isa. 11:11–12; Zeph. 2:1–2 and Ezek. 38–39 presupposes such a setting.

Zephaniah 1:14–18 is one of the most colorful descriptions of "the day of the LORD," which we commonly call the tribulation period. Zephaniah 2:1–2 says that there will be a worldwide regathering of Israel before the day of the LORD. "Gather yourselves together, yes, gather, O nation without shame, before the decree takes effect—the day passes like the chaff—before the burning anger of the LORD comes upon you, before the day of the LORD's anger comes upon you."

Ezekiel 20:33–38 sets forth a regathering that must take place before the tribulation. Here the Lord promises to bring back the nation of Israel "from the peoples and gather [them] from the lands where [they] are scattered, with a mighty hand and with an outstretched arm and with wrath poured out" (verse 34). "With wrath poured out" is a descriptive reference to the tribulation. In order for this to occur in history, Israel must be back in the land before the tribulation. This passage distinctly teaches that it is the Lord who is bringing them back, and the current nation of Israel is in the process of fulfilling this passage.

In a similar vein, two chapters later, Ezekiel receives yet another revelation about a future regathering of national Israel (Ezek. 22:17–22). This time, the

Lord is "going to gather [them] into the midst of Jeru-salem" (verse 19). Like a skilled metalworker, the Lord will use the fire of the tribulation to purge out the unfaithful. The Lord says He will "gather you [Israel] and blow on you with the fire of My wrath, and you will be melted in the midst of it" (verse 21). Once again, "My wrath" depicts the time of the tribulation. It also follows here that the nation must be regathered before that event can take place. The outcome of this event will be that the nation "will know that I, the LORD, have poured out My wrath on you" (verse 22).

Before these things can happen, Jews from all over the world must return to the land, just like we see happening with the modern state of Israel. This, of course, does not mean that *every* Jew in the world has to be back in the land. But it does clearly mean that many of the Jewish people must have returned to their ancient homeland. End-time prophecy in the Bible is built upon the assumption that Israel is both regath-ered to her land and is functioning as a nation.

The implications of Daniel 9:24–27 are unmistak-able. "And he [Antichrist] will make a firm covenant with the many for one week [one week of years or seven years]." In other words, the seven-year tribula-tion period will begin with the signing of a covenant between Antichrist and the leaders of Israel. Obviously, the signing of this treaty presupposes the presence of a Jewish leadership in a Jewish nation. This Jewish state must exist before a treaty can be signed.[296]

To summarize, then, the logic goes like this: The tribulation cannot begin until the seven-year covenant is made. The covenant cannot be put in place until a Jewish state exists. Therefore, a Jewish state must exist before the tribulation.

In view of all this, we believe that the main purpose for the regathering of Israel relates directly to the peace pact with Antichrist (Dan. 9:24–27). For such a treaty to be viable, the Jews have to be present in the land and organized into a political state. Since 1948 they have been nationally in the land of Israel. It is this modern miracle—something unheard of in history—that we, our parents, and our grandparents have witnessed unfolding before our eyes. An ancient and scattered people have returned to their ancestral homeland after almost two millennia, making the peace covenant of Daniel 9 possible for the first time since AD 70.[297]

As a result, the stage is set for the very event that will trigger the tribulation and usher in the final days of the world as we know it. Much to the disappointment of those who are opposed to Zionist theology, the modern state of Israel is in just such a position. This truly indicates that we are near the end of days.

## A Gathering in Stages

3) The Bible predicts that Israel's first regathering before the tribulation will occur in phases or stages.

In AD 70 the land of Israel, the city of Jerusalem, and the Jewish temple were crushed under the heel of Roman domination. Since that time, the Jews have primarily been spread out all over the world, even though a remnant has always existed in the land.[298]

God's warning of worldwide exile in Deuteronomy 28:64–66 has been literally and graphically fulfilled in the last nineteen hundred years:

> Moreover, the LORD will scatter you among all peoples, from one end of the earth to the other end of the earth; and there you shall serve other gods, wood and stone, which you or your fathers have not known. And among those nations you shall find no rest, and there shall be no resting place for the sole of your foot; but there the LORD will give you a trembling heart, failing of eyes, and despair of soul. So your life shall hang in doubt before you; and you shall be in dread night and day, and shall have no assurance of your life.

But as we have seen, the Bible predicts that Israel will return to the land in the end times. Scripture further indicates that this regathering will occur in stages.

In the famous "valley of dry bones" vision of Ezekiel 37:1–14, the bones symbolize the nation of Israel coming back together in the end times. In that passage, Ezekiel sees a graveyard vision illustrating the national return, restoration, and regeneration of "the whole house of Israel" (verse 11). Israel is first restored physically, and that restoration is pictured as bones, sinew, and skin coming together. The complete skeleton comes together bone by bone, joint by joint. But it is still a lifeless corpse (verse 8). Ezekiel calls this a work of the Lord (verse 14). If, as we believe, this word picture portrays the modern state of Israel, then this regathering since 1948 has certainly been a work of God and is biblically significant.

Following this regathering in unbelief, Ezekiel witnesses Israel's spiritual regeneration, as the Spirit breathes life into the dead nation (verse 9). Of course, this spiritual regeneration will not occur until just before Messiah returns.

We believe that the process of physical regathering to the land has begun. Preparations for the first worldwide regathering of Israel have been going on now for about 130 years. A pile of bones is beginning to come together and take shape. Let us consider what has happened so far.

The modern beginning of the return to the land goes back as early as 1871, when a few pioneering Jews began to trickle back. By 1881, about twenty-five thousand Jews had settled there joining the indigenous Jewish population. At the first Zionist congress in 1897, led by founder Theodore Herzl, the goal of reclaiming the land for the Jewish people was officially adopted. The progress, however, was agonizingly slow. By 1914, only eighty thousand Jews had moved into the land.

During World War I, the British sought support from the Jews for the war effort. On November 2, 1917, British Foreign Secretary Arthur J. Balfour issued what has become known as the Balfour Declaration. The declaration was contained in a letter from Balfour to Lord Rothschild, head of the Israel fund. In the letter, Balfour gave approval to the Jewish goal of reclamation: "His Majesty's government views with favor the establishment in Palestine of a national home for the Jewish people …."

In the face of persistent Arab pressure, however, and the desire of the British to maintain friendly relations with the Arabs, little was done in pursuit of the Balfour Declaration. Even so, it fanned into a flame Jewish hopes for the establishment of a homeland in the Holy Land—and encouraged more Jews to return. By 1939, when World War II broke out, about 450,000 Jews had managed to return to their homeland.

The Second World War and Nazi Germany's heinous, despicable treatment of the Jewish people created worldwide sympathy and a favorable environment for the Jewish people. Hitler's atrocities actually provided the greatest momentum for the establishment of a national homeland for the Jews. With United Nations approval, British control of the land ended on May 14, 1948. It was then a nation was reborn. At that time, Israel was given five thousand square miles of territory. It had a population of 650,000 Jews and several hundred thousand Arabs.

Since that historic day, further waves of immigrants have poured into Israel from all over the world, most notably from Ethiopia and the Soviet Union. By 2002, 37 percent of the 12.2 million Jews in the world were back in the land of Israel. To put this in perspective, in 1948 only 6 percent of the Jews in the world were in Israel. It is estimated that by the year 2030, half of the Jews worldwide will be back in the land. And it is happening before our very eyes, even though many have their eyes closed tight.

## The Final Scattering

4) The Jewish people will be scattered for the final time during the persecution of the Antichrist.

During the tribulation period, the Jewish people will be scattered over the face of the earth for the final time. With Antichrist in merciless pursuit, many will be killed, and many more will flee for their lives, becoming exiled and scattered across the globe (Dan. 7:25; Zech. 14:1–2; Matt. 24:15–21; Mark 13:14–20; Rev. 12).

## Second Worldwide Gathering in Belief

5) At the end of the tribulation, Israel will be regathered in belief, in preparation for the reign of Jesus Christ on earth.

As the tribulation grinds to its final, terrible moments, Jesus Christ will return from heaven to slay the Antichrist and his armies assembled in Israel for the final showdown. Then the Jewish people will be regathered to the land of Israel from all over the world for the second and final time, to rule and reign with their Messiah for one thousand years.

Many passages in the Bible speak of this final regathering. What a moment in history it will be! Israel will acknowledge their Messiah at His coming, the tribulation will be over, and the door to a glorious millennial kingdom will begin to swing open. Obviously, these references are not being fulfilled by the modern state of Israel today. Some of the citations for this notion include: Deut. 4:29–31; 30:1–10; Isa. 27:12–13; 43:5–7; Jer. 16:14–15; 31:7–10; Ezek. 11:14–18; Amos 9:14–15; Zech. 10:8–12; Matt. 24:31 . . . and many more.

God will use the unparalleled horror of the seven-year tribulation to bring many of the Jewish people to

BREAKING THE APOCALYPSE CODE

faith in the Lord Jesus as the Messiah of God, who died for their sins and rose again on the third day (Deut. 30:1–10; Jer. 31:27–34; Ezek. 36:22–32; Zech. 12:10–13:1).

We believe that this final return to the land will fulfill the prophetic aspects of the Feast of Trumpets (*Rosh Hashanah*) for the nation of Israel. This regathering requires a nation made up of those who are predominately believers in Jesus as their Messiah.

The reason the Jews must accept Jesus before He can return to earth is because of their rejection of Him at His first coming. According to Matthew 23:37, Christ will return to earth only when the nation of Israel, who spurned Him at His first coming, turns to Him in repentance and faith. In Matthew 23:37–39, He declared:

> O Jerusalem, Jerusalem, who kills the prophets and stones those who are sent to her! How often I wanted to gather your children together, the way a hen gathers her chicks under her wings, and you were unwilling. Behold, your house is being left to you desolate! For I say to you, from now on you shall not see Me until you say, "Blessed is He who comes in the name of the Lord!"

When Christ came to earth the first time, He offered the kingdom to the Jewish people, but they were unwilling to receive Him. Because of the nation's rejection of Jesus as their Messiah at His first coming, Christ now pronounces judgment upon them in verse 38 and says, "Behold, your house is being left to you desolate!"

What does He mean by "house"? It is a reference to the Jewish temple. Jesus continues His prophecy in 23:39: "For I say to you, from now on you shall not see Me until you say, 'Blessed is He who comes in the name of the Lord!'"

We see three key points in our Lord's statement. First, when He says, "from now on you will not see Me," Jesus speaks of His *departure*. Second, with the word *until*, He speaks of delay and postponement. Third, He looks to a time of Israel's future *repentance*, when just as they rejected Christ in the past, they will one day change their minds and realize that indeed Jesus is the nation's promised Messiah and will say, "Blessed is He who comes in the name of the Lord" (verse 39). This is the condition for the second coming described in the next chapter, Matthew 24. Fruchtenbaum further explains Matthew 23:39:

> But then He declares that they will not see Him again until they say, *Blessed is He that cometh in the name of the Lord*. This is a messianic greeting. It will mean their acceptance of the messiahship of Jesus.
>
> So Jesus will not come back to the earth until the Jews and the Jewish leaders ask Him to come back. For just as the Jewish leaders lead the nation to the rejection of the messiahship of Jesus, they must some day lead the nation to the acceptance of the messiahship of Jesus.[299]

Matthew 24:31 records a future regathering of Israel—this time in belief: "And He will send forth His angels with a great trumpet and they will gather together His elect from the four winds, from one end of the sky to the other." This will take place after the tribulation, in conjunction with the second coming (verse 29).

The final regathering is mentioned by the apostle Paul when he penned his section dealing with the nation of Israel (Rom. 9–11). Romans 10:13 declares concerning the Jewish people, "Whoever will call upon the name of the Lord will be saved." Paul then poses the question in verse 14: "How then shall they call upon Him in whom they have not believed? And how shall they believe in Him whom they have not heard? And how shall they hear without a preacher?" The point of Paul's reverse logic is that the Jews, within the context of the tribulation, cannot call upon Jesus to come rescue them from great tribulation if they do not believe in Him. Thus, in this passage, calling upon the Lord is in relation to physical salvation or deliverance from the threat of extinction at the hands of the armies of the world at Armageddon. Believing relates to spiritual salvation or the forgiveness of their sins through faith in Jesus as their Messiah. Thus, the second regathering requires belief on behalf of the nation's part.

Finally, all the prophecies about Israel's total possession and blessing in the land—going all the way back to God's original covenant with Abraham—will be fulfilled. And then these words of hope from the prophet Amos will come to pass: "'I will also plant them on their land, and they will not again be rooted out from their land which I have given them,' says the LORD your God" (9:15). This gathering will be final.

## Israel: God's Super Sign of the End Times

When we think about the unprecedented world-wide regathering and reestablishment of the nation of Israel, it prompts us to look more closely at *all* the international headlines. Now that Israel is poised in the very setting required for the revealing of Antichrist and the start of the tribulation, we begin to realize that prophetically significant events are happening all over the world. Even the renowned liberal theologian Karl Barth is reported to have said when Israel recaptured Jerusalem in 1967, "that the modern Christian must read with the Bible in one hand and the newspaper in the other."[300]

Walvoord says:

> **Of the many peculiar phenomena which characterize the present generation, few events can claim equal significance as far as biblical prophecy is concerned with that of the return of Israel to their land. It constitutes a preparation for the end of the age, the setting for the coming of the Lord for His church, and the fulfillment of Israel's prophetic destiny.[301]**

God has not—and will not—cast away His people. Israel is indeed God's "super sign" of the end times. She is the powder keg fuse for the final world conflict. And for the first time in almost two thousand years, the fuse is beginning to smolder. Zionism has been a tool used by God in history to get the snowball rolling downhill and now it cannot be stopped.

## CHAPTER eight

# THE TWO WITNESSES IN REVELATION 11

In his chapter on the historical principle of interpretation, Hanegraaff discusses the identity of the two witnesses in Revelation 11:3–13. Concerning their identity he says, "In like fashion, only someone with the background music of the Old Testament coursing through their mind comprehends that the two witnesses are a metaphorical reference to Moses and Elijah and reflect Old Testament jurisprudence that mandated at least two witnesses to convict of a crime (Deuteronomy 19:15)." He continues by noting that the two witnesses "represent the entire line of Hebrew prophets testifying against apostate Israel and preside over the soon-coming judgment and destruction of Jerusalem and the second temple" (13). But does this metaphorical view really come from the text itself or from Hanegraaff's imposition of his own view upon it?

## Zechariah 4 is the OT Background

Hanegraaff correctly observes that the Old Testament background for the two witnesses in Revelation 11 is Zechariah 4 and admits that the imagery in Zechariah 4 points to two literal individuals—Zerubbabel and Joshua—who led the returning remnant after the Babylonian captivity. The Old Testament imagery in

159

Zechariah 4 (two olive trees on either side of a lampstand) clearly refers to two individuals, Zerubbabel (the civil leader) and Joshua (the religious leader). When this same imagery is employed in Revelation 11 in conjunction with the two witnesses, doesn't it make sense that it would also refer to two individuals? Why is this so difficult to see? Why resort to a complicated "metaphorical reference" when the very Old Testament passage that forms the "background music" of Revelation 11 refers to two literal people? British Bible scholar W. Graham Scroggie, a well-known English pastor and commentator, states the issue plainly. "The mention of these two takes us back to Zechariah 4:3, 11, 14, from which we learn that they represented two individuals—Zerubbabel and Joshua. Therefore, in this passage also, they represent two individuals."[302] Yet, Hanegraaff ignores this clear Old Testament key to identifying the two witnesses and instead opts for an unnecessary metaphorical interpretation that he imposes upon the text.

In his discussion of the identity of the two witnesses, Hanegraaff says that one thing we must never do is "attempt to draw exact parallels between John's apocalyptic imagery and the scriptural referents from which they are drawn."[303] However, only ten pages earlier on page 122, Hanegraaff draws numerous exact parallels from Ezekiel 16 to prove that Jerusalem is Babylon in Revelation 17. But on page 132, when discussing Zechariah 4 and Revelation 11, he says that we should never do this. Again, this highlights Hanegraaff's inconsistency, and the fact that he really doesn't have a legitimate, consistent hermeneutical method.

Of the two witnesses Hanegraaff states that we must never "press the language system of Revelation into a literalistic labyrinth."[304] But he takes the temple in Revelation 11:1–2 as the literal second temple that was still standing when he believes Revelation was written. Then, when he comes to Revelation 11:3, the very next verse, he inexplicably switches hermeneutical gears and interprets the two witnesses metaphorically even though there is nothing within the text itself to signal this shift. Why is it a "literalistic labyrinth" to be consistent? If Hanegraaff is going to interpret the two witnesses metaphorically, why not interpret the temple metaphorically as well? Or, if he is going to interpret the temple literally, why not interpret the two witnesses the same way? Evidently, it is only a "literalistic labyrinth" if it doesn't fit Hanegraaff's view. It is much better to take the temple in Revelation 11:1–2 as a literal, future temple, the 1,260 days as a literal three-and-one-half year period of time during the future tribulation, and the two witnesses as two literal people who will serve God during this time of future tribulation. This maintains consistency and allows the text to speak for itself. Just as Satan will have his two henchmen on earth during the tribulation (the Beast and the False Prophet) so the Lord will have His two representatives on earth (the two witnesses) to counteract the evil of the Beast and the False Prophet.

## Eight Reasons the Two Witnesses are Literal, Future Individuals

Hanegraaff quickly dismisses the notion that the two

witnesses could be two literal individuals in the end times, especially two individuals from the past such as Moses and Elijah who are brought forward into the end times. However, the textual and historical evidence for this view is compelling. Eight key factors point to this view as the proper interpretation.

First, as already noted, the Old Testament background of Zechariah 4 points to the two witnesses as two literal individuals. Zechariah presents two witnesses (Zerubbabel and Joshua) who are pictured by a lampstand and an olive tree. The lampstand burned brightly and the olive tree produced oil which was burned in the candelabra. This picture is brought forward into Revelation 11 and reveals that these two end-time witnesses will shine in the darkness of the tribulation and will be fueled by the oil of the Holy Spirit.

Second, these two witnesses perform miracles that are identical to the ones performed by Moses and Elijah in the Old Testament. Moses and Elijah are both mentioned together in the final chapter of the Old Testament, and Malachi 4:5 says, "Behold, I am going to send you Elijah the prophet before the coming of the great and terrible day of the Lord." Moses and Elijah appeared with Jesus on the Mount of Transfiguration that prefigured Christ's second coming to earth (Matthew 17:1–5). It is consistent with the Old Testament for Elijah to make an appearance in the end times before the return of Christ (Malachi 4:5).

Third, Revelation 11:8 argues for a literal interpretation of the two witnesses. In this verse, the text explicitly states that the city of Jerusalem is figuratively called "Sodom and Egypt." The reader is not left to his own imagination to figure out what city is intended. It is clear in Revelation 11 that when God wants to speak figuratively or metaphorically He has no problem indicating that He is doing so. Since Revelation 11 does not say that the two witnesses are to be taken metaphorically or figuratively, one would assume they are to be taken literally as two prophets, just as they are described in the text.

Fourth, the Greek word *martur* (and *martus*), translated as "witness" or "witnesses," is found five times in Revelation and always refers to a literal person or persons. In Revelation 1:5 and 3:14 it refers to Jesus; in 2:13 it refers to Antipas; in 17:6 it refers to martyrs; and in 11:3 it refers to the two witnesses. Hanegraaff's "metaphorical reference" goes against the use of *martur* (witness) in Revelation in relation to literal individuals.

Fifth, the immediate context of Revelation 11 identifies the two witnesses. We need look no further than Revelation 11:10 which plainly identifies them as "these two prophets." How can this clear identification of the two witnesses be turned into a "metaphorical reference" and "represent the entire line of Hebrew prophets" as Hanegraaff suggests? Hanegraaff argues in *AC* that "soon" means soon, "near" means near, "you" means you, and so on. So, why doesn't "two prophets" mean two prophets? The words "these two prophets" identify the two witnesses as two individuals who will prophesy for God during the three-and-one-half year time of tribulation.

Sixth, Revelation 11:9–11 describes the amazing events that surround the death and resurrection of these two prophets. Revelation 11:9–11 says that they will be killed by the Beast when God lifts His hand of protection, that their bodies will be exposed in the streets of Jerusalem for three-and-one-half days, that "peoples and tribes and tongues and nations will look at their dead bodies," that after three-and-one-half days God will bring them back to life, that their enemies will see them resurrected and caught up to heaven and will be gripped with fear, and that in conjunction with their resurrection and rapture a great earthquake will occur that will destroy ten percent of Jerusalem and kill 7,000 people. Hanegraaff fails to adequately account for all these intricate details in his metaphorical interpretation. Again, it makes the best sense in the context to see the two witnesses as two future individuals who will literally fulfill these prophecies.[305]

Seventh, in the Old Testament book of Exodus Pharaoh serves as a kind of prototype of the future Beast or final Antichrist. Just as God had two witnesses, Moses and Aaron, who were the human instruments to call down the plagues on Pharaoh and Egypt, so God will use two literal witnesses in the end times to bring plagues (the trumpet judgments) down on the Beast and his empire.

Eighth, the view that the two witnesses are literal individuals in the end times is the consistent view of the early church. Hippolytus, in his treatise on the Antichrist, was one of the first, if not the first, to clearly identify the two witnesses. Hippolytus, who was the bishop of Rome from about AD 200–235, identified the two witnesses as Enoch and Elijah.[306] This view probably came about because neither of these men tasted physical death, and it was believed they had to return and die during the tribulation. Victorinus, who wrote the oldest extant Latin commentary on Revelation, died in AD 304. In his commentary on Revelation 11:3, he identified the two witnesses as two individuals who will preach for three-and-one-half years followed by the Antichrist's reign. The view that the two witnesses were Enoch and Elijah transported forward into the end times was held by Primasius, Andreas of Cappadocia, Arethas, and Adso of Montier-en-der.[307] The only variance from this view was from Lactantius, the most important apocalyptic writer of the early fourth century, who held that the two witnesses were a single end-time prophet. However, his view is still consistent with the notion that a literal prophet is in view.[308] The view that the two witnesses were Enoch and Elijah (or Enoch and Jeremiah) was so prevalent that historian LeRoy Froom says it was the view of the early church.[309] Bernard McGinn, in his work on the Antichrist, says that by the fourth century, "The standard Christian tradition, based on Apocalypse 11, had predicted two witnesses to preach before the coming of the final Antichrist."[310]

Hanegraaff rejects the view presented in *Left Behind* that the two witnesses are Moses and Elijah. He says, "Nor should we suppose that Moses and Elijah will be literally transported to the twenty-first century in a time machine."[311] While Hanegraaff may deride this notion, it was the unquestioned view of the early church that two prophets from the Old Testament would appear in the end times in conjunction with the appearance of the final Antichrist. While the early church believed the two witnesses would be Enoch and Elijah, others later identified them as Moses and Elijah. Many contemporary dispensationalists reject the idea that the two witnesses will be individuals from the past. They believe that the two witnesses will be two individuals God will raise up during the tribulation.[312] But, whatever specific view one adopts about the precise identity of the two witnesses, the one consistent thread in all these views is that the two witnesses will be two literal individuals who will prophesy in the end times.

## Conclusion

Hanegraaff's metaphorical view of the two witnesses exposes his inconsistent application of his hermeneutical principles. He cites Zechariah 4 as the Old Testament background for the two witnesses and then fails to follow his own "code" for interpreting Revelation in light of the Old Testament. He takes the temple in Revelation 11:1–2 as a reference to the literal temple in Jerusalem, and then without any textual signal to justify his shift, in the very next verse he interprets the two witnesses metaphorically. Why does he do this? Does this interpretation really come from the text or does it rise from his own view that he must read into the text? In *AC*, Hanegraaff warns, "When eschatological models are imposed on the text, the tapestry is undone and the loose ends dangle ignominiously."[313] Unfortunately, this is an apt description of what he does with Revelation 11 and the two witnesses.

The literal view of the two witnesses as two future prophets who will serve the Lord in the end times is consistent with a literal interpretation of the temple in Revelation 11:1–2, a literal interpretation of the three-and-one-half year time period in Revelation 11:2, the Old Testament background in Zechariah 4, the use of the word *martur* in Revelation, the immediate context where the two witnesses are clearly identified as "two prophets," the Old Testament parallel of Moses and Aaron calling down the plagues in Exodus 5–12, and the consistent view of the early church.

CHAPTER nine

# THE HARLOT IN REVELATION 17–18

The book of Revelation contains 404 verses, and 44 of these verses deal with Babylon (Rev. 14:8; 16:19; 17:1–18:24). That's about eleven percent of the entire book of Revelation devoted to one main topic—Babylon, the great harlot. One out of every nine verses in Revelation concerns Babylon. The fall of Babylon is announced in Revelation 14:8, briefly described in 16:19, and then given a thorough description in Revelation 17–18. The entire section of Revelation 17:1–19:10 is a single unit, with introductory and concluding formulas.[314]

In chapter 5 of *AC* (Historical Principle), Hanegraaff contends that the "harlot" city in Revelation 17 is the nation of Israel/the city of Jerusalem.[315] He presents his view of Babylon in Revelation 17 as a virtual slam dunk and wonders why others have missed what is so obvious to him. He says confidently, "What has puzzled me over the years is not the identity of the 'great prostitute,' but how so many could mistake her historical identity."[316] He then adds, "If the unveiling of the prostitute of Revelation . . . is so self-evident, why do so many prophecy teachers misidentify her? The answer once again lies in the maxim 'Error begets error.'"[317] Hanegraaff seems absolutely certain of this "self-evident" identification for Babylon. But is his certainty well-placed?

## Is Babylon Jerusalem?

To support his "self-evident" view that Babylon is Israel/Jerusalem, Hanegraaff provides two arguments. First, he notes that in Revelation 17, Babylon is referred to as a harlot. He then notes that in biblical history the only nation that is "inextricably linked to the moniker 'harlot'" is the nation of Israel.[318] Therefore, for him it is an open and shut case. The harlot in Revelation 17 must be apostate Israel and the city of Jerusalem. It is true that Israel is portrayed as a harlot, especially in Jeremiah and Ezekiel. However, as Hanegraaff mentions in a footnote, Nineveh is also called a harlot in the book of Nahum (3:4) as is the city of Tyre in Isaiah (23:15–16). The language of Revelation 17:2 is an allusion to the city of Tyre from Isaiah 23:17 where the harlotry is economic, not religious.[319] So, the harlot imagery is not as clear a link to Israel as Hanegraaff states.

Second, Hanegraaff says, "The biblical link between Ezekiel 16 and Revelation 17 in itself is enough to preclude misidentification."[320] He confidently, condescendingly says,

> **Ezekiel's depiction of apostate Israel as an insatiable prostitute is particularly significant in light of the self-evident parallels to Revelation .... A Sunday school child with a Bible in hand can find a hundred or more parallels on a quiet Sunday afternoon. Nowhere are the parallels more poignant than in Ezekiel 16 and Revelation 17—sequentially linked and memorable.**[321]

He then notes some of the similarities between Ezekiel 16 and Revelation 17.[322] While there are some parallels between these two texts, the Old Testament passage that most closely parallels Revelation 17–18 is Jeremiah 50–51, not Ezekiel 16. Jeremiah 50–51 is an Old Testament passage that describes the destruction of the literal city of Babylon on the Euphrates.

The first time Babylon is mentioned in Revelation is in 14:8 where the language closely parallels Jeremiah 51:7–8. From the outset, therefore, Babylon in Revelation is compared to ancient Babylon, not Israel or Jerusalem. Jeremiah 50–51 is a pair of chapters that serve as a kind of Old Testament counterpart to Revelation 17–18. Jeremiah 50–51 clearly describes the literal, geographical city of Babylon on the Euphrates. The many parallels between this passage and the future Babylon in Revelation 17–18 indicate that they are both describing the same city.

### PARALLELS BETWEEN JEREMIAH 50–51 AND REVELATION 17–18[323]

|  | Jeremiah 50–51 | Revelation 17–18 |
| --- | --- | --- |
| compared to a golden cup | 51:7a | 17:3–4; 18:6 |
| dwelling on many waters | 51:13a | 17:1 |
| involved with nations | 51:7b | 17:2 |
| named the same | 50:1 | 18:10 |
| destroyed suddenly | 51:8a | 18:8 |
| destroyed by fire | 51:30b | 17:16 |
| never to be inhabited | 50:39 | 18:21 |
| punished according to her works | 50:29 | 18:6 |
| fall illustrated | 51:63–64 | 18:21 |
| God's people flee | 51:6, 45 | 18:4 |
| heaven to rejoice | 51:48 | 18:20; 19:1 |
| not found any longer | 51:63–64 | 18:21 |

BREAKING THE APOCALYPSE CODE

There are several other clear allusions to ancient Babylon in Revelation 17–18. Revelation 18:5 says that Babylon's "sins have piled up as high as heaven, and God has remembered her iniquities." This is a clear allusion back to Genesis 11:4 where sinful man attempted to build a tower as high as heaven. Revelation 18:7 quotes Isaiah 47:5–7 which is another reference to the city of Babylon in the Old Testament. Revelation 18:22 refers back to Jeremiah 25:10 which also deals with ancient Babylon.

Hanegraaff consistently accuses dispensationalists of *eisegesis*, that is, "reading into the biblical text something that simply isn't there"[324] and heralds his new method he calls "e squared." However, this is another illustration of Hanegraaff's lack of exegesis. One wonders why Hanegraaff makes no mention of the numerous parallels between Jeremiah 50–51 and Revelation 17–18. Or why he fails to follow his own principle of "interpreting Scripture in light of Scripture." Babylon is the second most mentioned city in the Bible, trailing only the city of Jerusalem in frequency. Jerusalem is mentioned about 800 times, and Babylon is mentioned about 300 times. Every Old Testament mention of Babylon is a reference to the literal city on the Euphrates River. By the time one gets to Revelation there are hundreds of references to literal Babylon. A consistent pattern has been developed. To use Hanegraaff's language, "someone with the background music of the Old Testament coursing through their minds"[325] should know that in the Old Testament Babylon means Babylon (about 300 times), not Israel or Jerusalem.

## Babylon Means Babylon

Think about it. If the Old Testament is the key to decoding the book of Revelation, as Hanegraaff states, why would John suddenly change the established meaning of Babylon, which is reinforced about 300 times in the Old Testament, to Jerusalem the last time Babylon is mentioned in the Bible? No careful, informed reader could expect this sudden shift, this hermeneutical jolt, just a few chapters from the end of the Bible, yet this is what *AC* would have us believe.

Moreover, Revelation contains the names of many other geographical locations: Patmos, Ephesus, Smyrna, Pergamum, Thyatira, Sardis, Philadelphia, and Laodicea (see Revelation 1–3). These names are almost universally understood as the literal locations their names denote. Hanegraaff agrees that these are literal, geographical locations. Armageddon, which is mentioned in Revelation 16:16, is a literal place in northern Israel. The one time John wants to identify a geographical location using symbolic language, he alerts the reader to the fact that it is non-literal. In Revelation 11:8 he refers to Jerusalem as "Sodom and Egypt," but he makes it clear that he is not speaking literally: "The great city *which mystically is called* Sodom and Egypt" (italics added). John is being very careful here to let the reader know when he is not speaking literally of Sodom and Egypt. This indicates that when he leaves explanations of this sort out, he intends for us to take his words at face value.

In Revelation, the great city is specifically called "Babylon" six times (14:8; 16:19; 17:5; 18:2, 10, 21).

While it might be possible that the name "Babylon" is a code name for Rome, New York, Jerusalem, or some other city, there is no such indication in the text. And since the Bible itself doesn't imply that the term ought to be taken figuratively or symbolically, it is far safer to take it as referring to literal Babylon.

Henry Morris supports this literal understanding of Babylon. "It must be stressed again that *Revelation* means 'unveiling,' not 'veiling.' In the absence of any statement in the context to the contrary, therefore, we must assume that the term Babylon applies to the real city of Babylon, although it also may extend far beyond that to the whole system centered at Babylon as well."[326]

## Jerusalem Cannot be the Harlot of Revelation 17

One also wonders why Hanegraaff never considers the numerous obstacles to taking the harlot in Revelation 17 as Jerusalem. Proper exegesis would require at least an awareness of these problems. Here are a few.

- *Babylon must sit on many waters.* Jerusalem doesn't sit on many waters as required by Revelation 17:15 and 18:17–18. While the waters in 17:15 are identified as the nations of the world, it appears that this city is a major source of international sea trade (18:17–18).

- *Babylon must reign over the kings of the earth.* Revelation 17:18 says that the great city of Babylon reigns over the kings of the earth. Clearly, Jerusalem did not reign over the kings of the earth in AD 70. She did not even reign over herself in the first century. She was in political bondage to Rome. Babylon, which will serve as a capital city of the Antichrist in the end times, will rule over the nations.

• *Babylon must be the leading world economic center.* In the first century Jerusalem was never the world economic city described in Revelation 17–18. Even in one's wildest imagination, the city of Jerusalem in the first century cannot even come close to the description of Babylon as the economic juggernaut and hub of the world.

For these reasons, Hanegraaff's identification of Babylon in Revelation 17 as Jerusalem is not consistent with the text, with sound exegesis, or even with his own "code" of tethering our interpretations to the Old Testament, and therefore, must be rejected.

## CHAPTER ten

# UNDERSTANDING THE TIMES: "SOON" AND "NEAR"

One of the linchpins in Hanegraaff's interpretation of Revelation and his entire eschatological system is his insistence that the events in Revelation had to occur within a few years of the time Revelation was written. He bases this idea primarily on the occurrence of the words "soon" (*tachos*) and "near" (*engus*) in Revelation (1:1, 3). Hanegraaff says, "We interpret the Bible in accordance with the basic rules of language .... To say we are going to have dinner 'soon' could not possibly mean dinner in the distant future."[327] He continues, "Though LaHaye spiritualizes the meaning of 'soon' in the first verse of Revelation, there is no reason for anyone else to take it any way other than in its plain meaning and natural sense."[328]

We wholeheartedly agree that "soon" (*tachos*) and "near" (*engus*) should be understood in their plain meaning and natural sense, which is determined by usage and context. And as we will see, Hanegraaff doesn't even follow his own definition of "soon" and "near."

## "Soon" and "Near"

The noun *tachos* and the adverb *tachus* appear eight times in the Apocalypse (Revelation 1:1; 2:16; 3:11;

11:14; 22:6, 7, 12, 20). According to BDAG, which is the standard Greek lexicon, both words refer to "a very brief period of time, with focus on speed of an activity or event, speed, quickness, swiftness, haste."[329] The adverbial unit *en tachei* which appears in Rev 1:1 and 22:6 is defined as "soon, in a short time."[330]

"Near" (*engus*) occurs two times in the book of Revelation (1:3; 22:10) and is usually translated "near" or "at hand." It means "close proximity spatially" or "being close in point of time."[331] Based on the presence of these terms in Revelation 1:1 and 1:3, Hanegraaff insists that the events of Revelation had to be fulfilled within a few years of the time the book was written.

## Two Major Problems with Hanegraaff's View of "Soon" and "Near"

There are two fundamental problems with Hanegraaff's understanding of *tachos* and *engus* in Revelation. First, these timing statements are strategically located to frame the entire content of Revelation. Both *tachos* and *engus* occur at the very beginning of Revelation and again at the very end. The following chart depicts the strategic location of these terms in Revelation.

| Commencement of Revelation (1:1–8 is the Introduction) | Climax of Revelation (22:6–21 is the Conclusion) |
|---|---|
| *tachos* 1:1 | 22:6 (*tachos*) 22:7, 12, 20 (*tachus*) |
| *engus* 1:3 | 22:10 |

These timing terms are also emphasized by their repetition. They occur a total of seven times in the opening and closing chapters of Revelation. With these statements serving as bookends for the entire prophetic content of Revelation, whatever meaning one gives to these timing terms must be applied to all the events in the book.

Revelation 1:3      Blessed is he who reads and those who hear the words of the prophecy, and heed the things which are written in it; for the time is near.

Revelation 22:10   And he said to me, "Do not seal up the words of the prophecy of this book, for the time is near."

Vern Poythress notes, "But 1:3 and 22:10 are like bookends enclosing the whole prophecy of Revelation. The fulfillment of everything, not just a part, is near."[332] Thus, Hanegraaff's interpretation of these timing terms would require an AD 70 fulfillment of the entire Apocalypse, including 20:7–22:21, which he interprets as referring to events that are still future even today.[333]

Hanegraaff says, "Lest we be seduced into adding a great parenthesis of two thousand years between John's apocalyptic vision and the judgments the vision symbolizes, we should reread Revelation with an eye toward the words 'soon' and 'near.'"[334] Yet, after warning against this seduction, Hanegraaff, at the bottom of the very same page, says,

Likewise, we should never suppose that the imagery of Revelation is exhausted in a first-century historical milieu. For one day, the Lord Himself will come down from heaven, and the dwelling of God will forever be with men (Revelation 21:3); each person will be resurrected and 'judged according to what he has done' (20:13); and the problem of sin will be fully and finally resolved (21:27).

Thus, Hanegraaff himself adds "a great parenthesis of two thousand years."

Hanegraaff's own argument here works against him. Revelation 22:10 is a summary of the entire book and includes all of the content of Revelation when it says, "And he said to me, 'Do not seal up the words of the prophecy of this book, for the time is near.'" This means that everything in the entire prophecy of the book of Revelation must be "near." Hanegraaff can't legitimately say that the events in Revelation 1:1–20:6 were near and soon while the events in Revelation 20:7-22:21 were at least 2,000 years away. To maintain consistency in his view of soon and near, Hanegraaff must either adopt a view similar to futurism or shift to the extreme preterist view that understands the entire book of Revelation as past history and thus eliminates any future second coming and resurrection. However, since full or radical preterism denies a literal second coming of Christ and the future bodily resurrection, it is outside the pale of orthodoxy and is not a legitimate option. Thus, one is left with futurism as the only credible, consistent option. In short, the inconsistency of Hanegraaff's partial preterist approach to the timing texts undermines the validity of this view.

In what sense did the final release of Satan (Rev. 20:7-9) and the final judgment (Rev 20:11-15) begin soon after Revelation was composed? They did not. They are removed from AD 95 by over 1,900 years. Hanegraaff's view goes against his own warning not to be "seduced into adding a great parenthesis of two thousand years between John's apocalyptic vision and the judgments which the vision symbolizes" (160). The failure of this view of the timing texts to account for all the events in Revelation within a chronological nearness renders this view invalid.

Second, the Apocalypse is described as a prophecy in 1:3 and 22:7. Yet, if Revelation was written in AD 65–66 and Rev. 1:1–20:6 was fulfilled "soon" in the events of AD 64–70 as partial preterists maintain, then the bulk of the book was already fulfilled before most Christians ever heard or read its contents. By the time the book was written by John on Patmos in AD 65–66, copied, and carried by the messengers of the seven churches, and then re-copied and widely disseminated, the prophesied events would have already occurred. The powerful prophetic message of the Apocalypse would have been one great anti-climax. By the time most people heard the message of the book, the "soon" events of AD 70 would have already occurred. Revelation would have had one of the shortest shelf-lives of any book in history.

Therefore, Hanegraaff's view of the timing terms in Revelation should be rejected. But if this interpretation of the timing texts is invalid, how should they be understood? If one adopts a futurist view of Rev. 4–22 how could events so remotely future be legitimately described as "soon" or "at hand"?

## The Imminency View

It seems best to understand the timing terms in Revelation in relation to the prophetic viewpoint of the author and not as necessarily meaning that the events had to occur within a few years of the time Revelation was written. The New Testament authors consistently describe this present age, or the time between the two comings, as the "last days" or "latter days."[335] This attitude is expressed in 1 John 2:18 where the present age is even designated as the "last hour."[336] This means that the "last days" and even the "last hour" have been ongoing for over 1,900 years. The phrase in 1 John 2:18 is especially significant because it originated from the same author as Revelation and provides further insight into the apostle John's prophetic viewpoint.

The phrases "last days" and "last hour" both carry an eschatological dimension. Every generation of believers, including the present one, have lived in times that strongly cry out the sense of impending and overhanging destiny.[337] The last of these last days is always imminent or impending.[338] Since no man knows God's time schedule, the time of fulfillment is always "at hand." These events are near, in that, they are the next events on God's prophetic calendar. There is a nearness, next-ness, or at-hand-ness of the time.[339] As Robert Thomas notes, "The purpose of *en tachei* is to teach the imminence of the events foretold, not to set a time limit in which they must occur."[340] The imminency of these events, emphasized in Revelation from its commencement to its close, calls each generation to an attitude of expectancy and readiness.[341] The imminent expectancy and the necessity of readiness is expressed by Jesus repeatedly in the Olivet Discourse (Matthew 24:36, 42, 44; 25:10–13). Poythress concludes that biblical prophecy focuses "more on the character of the times. Jesus' exhortations to watch (Mark 13:32–37) do not depend on whether the second coming is five days away or five millennia away, but on the responsibility of the disciples after He, the Master, 'leaves His house.'"[342]

New Testament scholar Robert Mounce favors the imminency view of the timing statements in Revelation:

> **The most satisfying solution is to take the expression "must soon take place" in a straightforward sense, remembering that in the prophetic outlook the end is always imminent. Time as chronological sequence is of secondary concern in prophecy. This perspective is common to the entire New Testament. Jesus taught that God would vindicate His elect without delay (Luke 18:8), and Paul wrote to the Romans that God would "soon" crush Satan under their feet (Rom. 16:20).[343]**

First Peter 4:7, which says, "The end of all things is at hand; therefore, be of sound judgment and sober spirit for the purpose of prayer," is another New Testament text that uses the language of imminence to draw the reader into a sense of expectation, motivation, and responsibility.[344] Alan Johnson agrees with Mounce:

In eschatology and apocalyptic, the future is always viewed as imminent without the necessity of intervening time (cf. Luke 18:8) …. Therefore, "soonness" means imminency in eschatological terms. The church in every age has always lived with the expectancy of the consummation of all things in its day. Imminency describes an event possible any day, impossible no day.[345]

George Ladd also supports this view:

The problem is raised by the fact that the prophets were little interested in chronology, and the future was always viewed as imminent. Biblical prophecy is not primarily three-dimensional but two; it has height and breadth but is little concerned about depth, i.e., the chronology of future events. There is in biblical prophecy a tension between the immediate and distant future; the distant is viewed through the transparency of the immediate. It is true that the early church lived in expectancy of the return of the Lord, and it is the nature of biblical prophecy to make it possible for every generation to live in expectancy of the end. To relax and say, "Where is the promise of His coming?" is to become a scoffer of divine truth. The "biblical" attitude is "take heed, for you do not know when the time will come" (Mark 13:33).[346]

When the time texts of Revelation are understood in light of the prophetic viewpoint of the author, the nature of the entire church age in the New Testament as the "last hour," and the ever-present, overhanging imminency of the end times, it is clear that they are not intended to indicate events that were necessarily a few years away when it was written.

UNDERSTANDING THE TIMES: "SOON" AND "NEAR"

## Conclusion

Hanegraaff repeatedly holds the words "soon" and "near" in Revelation to mean that the prophecies in the book had to occur within a few years of the time of its writing. He says, "When Jesus said 'this generation,' He did not mean *that*; when He used the pronoun *you*, His hearers knew precisely who He was talking about; and when He said 'soon,' His servants did not suppose He was referencing a time twenty-one centuries future . . . " However, Hanegraaff says clearly that some of the events in the book are still future. So, according to his view, "soon" and "near" only mean soon and near for part of the book. But how does Hanegraaff know what parts were fulfilled in AD 70 and what parts are still unfulfilled? Without any legitimate exegetical justification, he makes the 1,900-year leap in the middle of Revelation 20. If he is going to push some of the events in Revelation into the distant future, why not put all the events in Revelation 4–22 there? This is the futurist position. This is the consistent position.

Hanegraaff's interpretation of "soon" and "near" is another example of the failed method and model presented in *AC*.

## CHAPTER eleven

# WHEN WAS REVELATION WRITTEN?

*For LaHaye, everything hinges on proving that the book of
Revelation was written long after the destruction of the temple in
AD 70. If, like the rest of Scripture, Revelation was written prior
to AD 70, his entire* Left Behind *juggernaut is compromised.*

—Hank Hanegraaff, *The Apocalypse Code,* 109

The above statement by Hanegraaff is simply not accurate.
Hanegraaff acts as if a futurist interpretation of Revelation
is somehow dependent on an AD 95 date, which is not true.
However, it is true that Hanegraaff's view of Revelation
1:1–20:6 is totally dependent on a mid-sixties date for
Revelation. But he is *incorrect* in saying that a futurist view
of Revelation hinges on the mid-nineties date for the book.
Futurism is not based on any particular date of Revelation.
It is true that most futurists hold the AD 95 date, but this
is simply because they believe it is the correct date, not
because the view itself is dependent on that date. Former
Dallas Seminary professor Zane Hodges is a futurist, and
holds to a pre-AD 70 date for Revelation.

The primary interest of futurists in the date of
Revelation is not that a particular date is necessary to

undergird our view, but that the traditional AD 95 date, or any date after AD 70, is fatal to Hanegraaff's partial preterist view. As Francis Gumerlock notes, "Futurists, on the other hand, generally believe that the book of Revelation contains prophecies, the majority of which will be fulfilled near the end of the world. While a late date of Revelation is not crucial to their interpretation of the book, it is important in their polemic against preterism."[347] Richard Mayhue captures the importance of the date of Revelation to preterism in these words: "Significantly, a futurist would not have to change his eschatological thinking if a pre-AD 70 date for the writing were to be established. However, the preterist position is eliminated from consideration if the late date of ca. AD 95 can be validated."[348]

The mid-sixties date for the writing of the book of Revelation is a key component of Hanegraaff's view. He maintains that Revelation was written in about AD 65 during the reign of the Roman Emperor Nero. Hanegraaff also believes that the events in Revelation 1–19 were fulfilled in the events before and during the conquest of Israel by the Romans in AD 70. Since Revelation is a prediction of the future (1:1, 3, 11, 19; 22:6–10, 16, 18–20), if it was fulfilled by August AD 70, then obviously it had to be written by AD 65 or 66 even to be a possibility.

The problem for Hanegraaff is if Revelation was written after AD 70, then his view falls flat. The centrality of this issue to Hanegraaff's entire system can be seen from the fact that he discusses the date of Revelation many different times in *AC* (8, 109–110, 123–124,

WHEN WAS REVELATION WRITTEN?

152–160, 242n13, 255n43, 259–260n112, 260n115). That's why Hanegraaff and others like him who interpret much of Revelation preteristically (as already fulfilled in the events of AD 64–70) have to defend the mid-sixties date of Revelation so vigorously and without budging an inch. If they budge, their entire eschatological system collapses like a house of cards. The stubborn problem for Hanegraaff is that the evidence is strongly in favor of a date in the mid-nineties, thirty years too late for most of his interpretation of Revelation to stand.

The evidence for determining when the book of Revelation, or any biblical book, was written is divided into two main categories: external evidence (evidence from outside the book of Revelation) and internal evidence (evidence from within the book of Revelation itself). Let us examine these two lines of evidence and see what they tell us about the date of Revelation. We will begin with the external evidence, and you will see that there is a great deal Hanegraaff does not tell you in *AC*.[349]

## EXTERNAL EVIDENCE

### *Irenaeus—Exhibit A*

Hanegraaff's discussion of the external evidence for dating Revelation is very scant. This is not surprising since there is no early external evidence to support his view. No one supported the mid-sixties date of Revelation until the sixth century AD.

It is generally agreed that Irenaeus, the Bishop of Lyon, is "Exhibit A" for the dating of Revelation.[350] Irenaeus grew up in Smyrna, one of the cities where the book of Revelation was first circulated. He was also a disciple of Polycarp, who in turn was a disciple of the apostle John. There is a direct geographical and personal link between the author of Revelation and Irenaeus. A more qualified, knowledgeable witness for the date of Revelation could hardly be imagined.

In his classic work *Against Heresies*, written in about AD 180, Irenaeus says that the *apocalypse* or apocalyptic vision was seen near the end of the reign of the Roman Emperor Domitian, whose reign ended in AD 96. Here is the exact statement by Irenaeus:

> **But if it had been necessary to announce his name plainly at the present time, it would have been spoken by him who saw the apocalypse. For it was not seen long ago, but almost in our own time, at the end of the reign of Domitian.**[351]

Hanegraaff makes two arguments to try to get rid of this statement that puts a stake in the heart of his view. First, he says that the statement by Irenaeus is "markedly ambiguous."[352] He says that, "Because of the complexity of the Greek grammar, the sentence can be translated as saying that either *John* or John's *apocalyptic vision* was seen toward the end of Domitian's reign."[353] However, the statement is as straightforward and unambiguous as one could make it. Irenaeus says that the "apocalyptic vision" was seen toward the end of Domitian's reign, that is, in AD 95 or 96 since Domitian was assassinated in Rome on September 18, AD 96. It is not a complex Greek sentence. The word *apocalypse* is the nearest gram-matical antecedent to the verb "seen." Throughout the book, Hanegraaff argues for taking statements in their plain, normal meaning, for not "reading into the biblical text something that simply isn't there." Applying this maxim, and the simple rules of grammar, to the statement of Irenaeus, it is clear that he believed John saw the apocalyptic vision in AD 95–96. In further support of the clarity of Irenaeus' statement, it is interesting to note that the first person to question what he meant was a German preterist named Johann Jacob Wettstein in 1752.[354] For over 1,600 years the church had no problem understanding what Irenaeus meant. The alleged ambiguity in Irenaeus' statement has been created by modern preterists with a viewpoint that demands a pre-70 date for Revelation. In this case the maxim is true that "necessity is the mother of invention." Irenaeus' statement only becomes unclear and ambiguous if one has a problem with dating Revelation in AD 95.

Secondly, Hanegraaff calls the credibility of Irenaeus into question by noting that Irenaeus believed that Jesus was about fifty years old when He was crucified.[355] It is true that Irenaeus mistakenly held that Jesus was in His forties when He died, but this view was based on his interpretation of John 8:52–59.[356] There is an important distinction between these two issues. Irenaeus' view about the age of Jesus was based on an interpretation of a biblical text, whereas, the date of Revelation is a historical fact. It is much easier to misinterpret a biblical text than it is to misstate a historical fact. Irenaeus knew when Revelation was written based on first-hand testimony received from Polycarp. The clear testimony should be received and accepted.

191

There is another interesting angle to this matter of the credibility of Irenaeus. Hanegraaff calls the credibility of Irenaeus into question concerning the date of Revelation on page 153 of *AC*. However, just thirteen pages earlier, on page 140, he cites Irenaeus to support the view that the apostle John was the author of Revelation. This is blatantly inconsistent. Why is Irenaeus reliable to tell us who wrote Revelation, but not reliable to tell us when it was written?[357] As Dr. Norman Geisler used to say in class at Dallas Theological Seminary, "What's sauce for the goose is sauce for the gander." This kind of selective "cherry picking" to support one's view is hypocritical and betrays a serious lack of scholarship.

## More Early Witnesses for the AD 95 Date

While Irenaeus is "Exhibit A" for the AD 95 date of Revelation, he is certainly not alone. In addition to the testimony of Irenaeus, there is a long, uninterrupted line of witnesses for the AD 95 date of Revelation. Hanegraaff contends that the AD 95 date of Revelation is "largely dependent on a single, and markedly ambiguous, sentence in the writings of Irenaeus, bishop of Lyons."[358] This is simply not accurate. Thirty years before Irenaeus, Hegesippus held to the late date of Revelation.[359] Here are some of the other witnesses for the AD 95 date of Revelation.

### Clement of Alexandria (ca. 155–220)

Titus Flavius Clemens or Clement of Alexandria is known as the Father of Alexandrian Christianity. He was the head of the Catechetical School of Alexandria. The following is Clement's statement concerning the date of Revelation.

**And to give you confidence, when you have thus truly repented, that there remains for you a trustworthy hope for salvation, hear a story that is no mere story, but a true account of John the apostle that has been handed down and preserved in memory. When after the death of the tyrant he removed from the island of Patmos to Ephesus, he used to journey by request to the neighboring districts of the Gentiles, in some places to appoint bishops, in others to regulate whole churches, in others to set among the clergy some one man, it may be, of those indicated by the Spirit.**[360]

Notice that Clement references a "true account of John the apostle that has been handed down and preserved in memory." He is clearly referring to some well-known tradition in the church. The only tradition that had been handed down and preserved at that time was the tradition that Revelation was written during the reign of Domitian. Had Clement intended someone other than Domitian, he no doubt would have named that person specifically in light of the established tradition of John's banishment under Domitian. Additionally, Eusebius understood that Clement meant Domitian when he referred to the tyrant citing him along with Irenaeus as a witness.

*Origen (ca. 185–254)*
Origenes Adamantius, better known as Origen, was a disciple of Clement of Alexandria. Origen's relevant statement on the date of Revelation came from comments he made on Matthew 16:6. In those comments he said, "The king of the Romans, as tradition teaches, condemned John, who bore

testimony, on account of the word of truth, to the isle of Patmos."[361] The difficulty in this statement, as with Clement of Alexandria, is that Origen does not identify who he means by "the king of the Romans." However, the phrase "as tradition teaches" points to Domitian as the king of the Romans because the tradition to which Origen alludes must have been handed down from Hegesippus and Irenaeus because at this time there was no other settled tradition in the church. Knowing this tradition, had Origen intended someone other than Domitian he most likely would have named that person to correct any perceived mistake.

### Victorinus (died AD 304)

Victorinus was the bishop of Pettau in Pannonia. He wrote the earliest known Latin commentary on Revelation. He is widely recognized as the first great exegete of the Western church. Victorinus suffered martyrdom under the Roman Emperor Diocletian. His commentary on the Apocalypse holds the honor of being the oldest extant commentary on Revelation. As a commentator on the Apocalypse, one can assume that he took a great interest in the date the book was written. Victorinus made two statements in his commentary in support of the AD 95 date of Revelation.

First, in his *Commentary on the Apocalypse* at Revelation 10:11, he noted:

> He says this, because when John said these things he was in the island of Patmos, condemned to the labor of the mines by Caesar Domitian. There, therefore, he saw the Apocalypse; and when grown old, he thought

**that he should at length receive his quittance by suffering, Domitian being killed, all his judgments were discharged. And John being dismissed from the mines, thus subsequently delivered the same Apocalypse which he had received from God.**[362]

Secondly, commenting further upon Revelation 17:10, Victorinus states, "The time must be understood in which the written Apocalypse was published, since then reigned Caesar Domitian."[363] The plain, uncontroverted testimony of Victorinus adds another strong plank of support to the Domitianic date of Revelation.

*Eusebius (ca. 260–340)*
Eusebius was bishop of Caesarea in Israel, and is known as "the father of church history" due to his classic work *Ecclesiastical History*. Several times in his writings he expressly dated the Apocalypse to the reign of Domitian.[364] He even specifically dated John's banishment to Patmos in AD 95.[365] His witness is especially weighty because he had much of the early Christian literature at his disposal. Apparently, he was not even aware of a contrary tradition to the AD 95 date.

*Jerome (ca. 331–420)*
Jerome was a giant of the ancient church. He is recognized as the most learned man in the Latin-speaking church of the late fourth century.[366] He was born at Stridon in Dalmatia and Pannonia about AD 331. Jerome was proficient in several languages. His literary accomplishments were prolific. At the direction of Pope Damascus, he translated the Scripture into Latin

(the Vulgate). In 386 he settled in Bethlehem where he died on September 30, 420. In two places Jerome stated clearly that John was banished to the island of Patmos during the reign of the Roman Emperor Domitian. First, in his *Against Jovinianus* (AD 393), Jerome wrote:

> **John is both an apostle and an evangelist, and a prophet. An apostle, because he wrote to the churches as a master; and evangelist, because he composed a gospel, a thing which no other of the apostles, excepting Matthew, did; a prophet, for he saw in the island of Patmos, to which he had been banished by the Emperor Domitian as a martyr for the Lord, an Apocalypse containing boundless mysteries of the future.**[367]

Secondly, Jerome's most specific statement is found in his *Lives of Illustrious Men*, where he writes about John's banishment.

In the fourteenth year then after Nero, Domitian having raised a second persecution, he was banished to the island of Patmos, and wrote the Apocalypse, on which Justin Martyr and Irenaeus afterwards wrote commentaries. But Domitian having been put to death and his acts, on account of his excessive cruelty, having been annulled by the senate, he returned to Ephesus under Pertinax and continuing there until the time of the emperor Trajan, founded and built churches throughout all Asia, and, worn out by old age, died in the sixty-eighth year after our Lord's passion and was buried near the same city.[368]

Jerome is another strong link in the steady chain of late-date supporters for Revelation.

Here is the external evidence for the date of Revelation side by side. You be the judge!

### SUMMARY OF THE EXTERNAL EVIDENCE

| Witnesses for the Domitianic Date (AD 95) | Witnesses for the Neronic Date (AD 65) |
|---|---|
| Hegesippus (150 AD) | |
| Irenaeus (AD 180) | |
| Clement of Alexandria (ca. 155–220) | |
| Origen (ca. 185–254) | |
| Victorinus (ca. 300) | |
| Eusebius (ca. 300) | |
| Jerome (ca. 400) | |
| Sulpicius Severus (ca. 400) | |
| The Acts of John (ca. 650) | |
| Primasius (ca. 540) | Syriac Version of NT (508 and 616) |
| Paulus Orosius (ca. 600) | |
| Andreas (ca. 600) | |
| Venerable Bede (ca. 700) | |
| | Arethas (ca. 900) |
| | Theophylact (d. 1107) |

As you can see, by placing the external evidence side by side, the first clear, accepted, unambiguous witness to the Neronic date for Revelation is a one-line subscription in the Syriac translation of the New Testament in AD 508 and then in another version in AD 616. There are only two other external witnesses to the mid-sixties date: Arethas (c. 900) and Theophylact (d. 1107).

The late date, on the other hand, has an unbroken line of support from some of the greatest, most reliable names in church history beginning in AD 150. The external evidence from church history points emphatically and overwhelmingly to the AD 95 date for the composition of Revelation.

## INTERNAL EVIDENCE

In considering the internal evidence for the date of Revelation, let's begin by examining Hanegraaff's arguments and then look at the evidence for the AD 95 date.

# Hanegraaff's Three Towers

Hanegraaff identifies "three arguments that tower above the rest"[369] in his attempt to defend the AD 65 date for Revelation. Let us look at these three towers and see if they are built on stone or sand.

### Tower 1: No mention of the destruction of Jerusalem in Revelation

Hanegraaff's first tower is an argument from silence. He says, "Just as it is unreasonable to suppose that someone writing a history of the World Trade Center in the aftermath of September 11, 2001, would fail to mention the destruction of the Twin Towers, so too it stretches credulity to suggest that Revelation was written in the aftermath of the devastation of Jerusalem and the Jewish temple and yet makes no mention of this apocalypse."[370] One must remember that Revelation was written to a primarily Gentile audience in Asia Minor, about 800 miles from Jerusalem, 25 years after AD 70. The original audience was removed ethnically, geographically, and chronologically from the destruction of Jerusalem. Also, Revelation says clearly that it is a prophecy about the future (1:3; 22:10) and not history as Hanegraaff supposes. The simple reason John didn't record the events of AD 70 is that it was a past event, and Revelation is a prophecy.

In discussing this point, Hanegraaff quotes Norman Geisler to support his view. Yet, Geisler, in a review of *AC*, states that he has held to the AD 95 date of Revelation for 50 years. He said that *AC* "takes a quote from our book out of context . . . I never said any such thing .... I never said, nor do I believe that John wrote Revelation before AD 70."[371]

## Tower 2: No mention in Revelation of the fulfillment of Jesus' prophecy of the destruction of Jerusalem

Hanegraaff's second tower is another argument from silence. He says,

> As the student of the New Testament well knows, New Testament writers were quick to highlight fulfilled prophecy. The phrase "This was to fulfill what was spoken of by the prophets" permeates the pages of Scripture and demonstrates conclusively that the Bible is divine rather than human in origin. Thus, it is inconceivable that Jesus would make an apocalyptic prophecy concerning the destruction of Jerusalem and the Jewish temple and that John would fail to mention that the prophecy was fulfilled one generation later just as Jesus predicted it.[372]

Hanegraaff says that "New Testament writers were quick to highlight fulfilled prophecies." However, it is generally agreed among scholars that the book of Revelation never *directly* quotes any previous prophecies. According to most counts, there are at least 278 allusions to the Old Testament in the 404 verses of Revelation. Yet, contrary to Hanegraaff's statement, Revelation never says, "This was to fulfill what was spoken by the prophets." Since Revelation does not directly state that any prophecy is being fulfilled, why does it surprise Hanegraaff that the prophecy of Jesus is not singled out?

### *Tower 3: John mentions a temple in Revelation 11:1–2*

Hanegraaff's third tower in defense of the early date of Revelation is based on the mention of a temple in Revelation 11:1–2. Hanegraaff says, "New Testament documents—including the book of Revelation—speak of Jerusalem and the Jewish temple intact at the time they were written."[373] Hanegraaff's insistence that the temple in Revelation 11:1–2 must be standing when John wrote, is surprising in view of the fact that he says the Old Testament is the key to understanding the book of Revelation. In the Old Testament books of Daniel and Ezekiel, both prophets describe future temples that did not exist at the time they wrote (Daniel 9:26–27; Ezekiel 40–48). When Daniel wrote, the Jewish temple was in ruins in Jerusalem. Likewise, when Ezekiel prophesied there was no temple standing in Jerusalem. If the Old Testament is the key or "code" for understanding the book of Revelation as Hanegraaff says, then one would expect John to also mention a future temple in his writings. And that is exactly what we find in Revelation 11:1–2. The temple in Revelation 11:1–2, in the context, is a future, third Jewish temple that will be rebuilt and desecrated by the coming Beast or Man of sin (Revelation 11:2; 2 Thessalonians 2:4).

It is also interesting that Hanegraaff insists that the temple in Revelation 11:1–2 must be the literal, second Jewish temple that was standing before its destruction in AD 70. Yet, in Revelation 11:3–11, without any signal in the text, he shifts to a metaphorical interpretation of the two witnesses. This fluid hermeneutic that is not moored to the text is not, as Hanegraaff loves to say, "reading the Bible for all its worth."

## INTERNAL EVIDENCE FOR THE AD 95 DATE

# The Condition of the Seven Churches

One of the key internal arguments for the late date of Revelation is the condition of the seven churches of Asia Minor in Revelation 2–3. The churches of Asia Minor show all the symptoms of the second generation. The period of Paul's great mission seems to lie in the past. Let us consider the clues on the date of Revelation from three of the churches addressed in Revelation 2–3.

### Church of Ephesus

If John wrote Revelation in AD 64–67, then the letter to the church of Ephesus in Revelation 2:1–7 overlaps with Paul's two letters to Timothy who was the pastor of the church when Paul wrote to him. In fact, if Revelation was written in 64–66, then it is very likely that Paul wrote 2 Timothy after John wrote to the church. Yet Paul makes no mention of the loss of first love or the presence of the Nicolaitans at Ephesus in his correspondence with Timothy. Neither does he mention these problems in his Ephesian epistle which was probably written in AD 62. Jesus' statement to the church of Ephesus in Revelation 2:2 that it had guarded itself well against error does not fit what we know of this church in Nero's day (Acts 20:29–30; 1 Tim. 1:3–7; 2 Tim. 2:17–18).

Those who support the early date often respond to this point by noting that error can erupt very quickly in a church. As an example they sometimes cite the churches of Galatia who Paul says, "so quickly deserted the gospel." But there is a great difference between the condition and maturity of the Galatian churches after Paul's brief visit there on his first missionary journey, and the church of Ephesus where Paul headquartered for three years, where Apollos taught, where Priscilla and Aquila ministered, and where Timothy pastored for several years.

Moreover, Revelation 2:1–7 makes no mention of the great missionary work of Paul in Asia Minor. On his third missionary journey Paul headquartered in Ephesus for three years and had a profound ministry there. If John wrote Revelation in AD 65 then the omission of any mention of Paul in the letters to the seven churches of Asia Minor is inexplicable. However, if John wrote thirty years later to the second generation in the churches, then the omission is easily understood.

## Church of Smyrna

Apparently, the church of Smyrna did not even exist during the ministry of Paul. Polycarp was the bishop of Smyrna. In his letter to the Philippians (11.3), written in about AD 110, Polycarp says that the Smyrnaeans did not know the Lord during the time Paul was ministering.

> But I have not observed or heard of any such thing among you, in whose midst the blessed Paul labored, and who were his letters of recommendation in the beginning. For he boasts about you in all the churches—those alone, that is, which at that time had come to know the Lord, for we had not yet come to know him.

Polycarp is saying that Paul praised the Philippian believers in all the churches, but that during Paul's ministry in the AD 50s and 60s the church of Smyrna did not even exist. As R. H. Charles, a scholar who specialized in book of Revelation studies, concludes:

> The church of Smyrna did not exist in 60–64 AD—at a time when St. Paul was boasting of the Philippians in all the churches. Cf. Polycarp. But though Polycarp's letter tells us that the church of Smyrna was not founded in 60–64 AD, he gives no hint as to when it was founded. Hence several years may have elapsed after that date before it was founded. When, however, we turn to Rev. 2:8–11 we find that our text presupposes a church poor in wealth but rich in good works, with a development of apparently many years to its credit. This letter, then, may have been written in the closing years of Vespasian (75–79) but hardly earlier.[374]

This evidence points to the close of the first century as the time of composition for Revelation.

### Church of Laodicea

The church of Laodicea is the only one of the seven churches (and possibly Sardis) that does not have one thing to commend. In his letter to the Colossians, probably written in AD 60–62, Paul indicates that the church was an active group (Colossians 4:13). He mentions the church there three times in his Colossian letter (2:2; 4:13, 16). It would certainly take more than three to five years for the church to depart so completely from its earlier acceptable status that absolutely nothing good could be said about it.

Laodicea is also described in Revelation as flourishing economically. Jesus quotes the church as saying, "'I am rich, and have become wealthy, and have need of nothing'" (Rev. 3:14–22). Yet the city suffered devastation in the earthquake of AD 60 or possibly 61. After the earthquake the Laodiceans refused all aid and assistance from Rome preferring to rebuild their devastated city from their own resources.

Tacitus, the Roman historian, in his *Annals* 14.27, describes this independent spirit. "In the same year, Laodicea, one of the famous Asiatic cities, was laid in ruins by an earthquake, but recovered by its own resources, without assistance from ourselves." The extent of the damage to Laodicea and the length of time it took to reconstruct the city are powerful evidences of the late date for Revelation.

Most of the main ruins that survive today in Laodicea are from buildings constructed during the time of earthquake reconstruction. The great public buildings destroyed in the earthquake were rebuilt at the expense of individual citizens and were not finished until about the year AD 90. The completion date of the stadium can be precisely dated to the latter part of AD 79 and the inscriptions on several other buildings indicate that they too can be dated to this same period. New gates and fortifications seem to have culminated the rebuilding of Laodicea. It is likely that the great triple gate (Syrian gate) and towers were not finished until AD 88–90.[375] The French archaeological team who conducted excavations at Laodicea in 1961–63 concluded that the reconstruction process after the earthquake covered a span of at least twenty years.[376]

Since the rebuilding of Laodicea after the earthquake occupied a complete generation, it is highly problematic to claim that Laodicea was rich, wealthy, and in need of nothing in AD 65. At that time, the city was in the early stages of a rebuilding program that would last another twenty-five years. However, if Revelation were written in AD 95 the description of Laodicea in Revelation 3:14–22 would fit the situation exactly. By this time the city was completely rebuilt with its own resources enjoying prosperity and prestige and basking in the pride of its great accomplishment.

## "Oil and Wine" in Revelation 6:6

Another internal argument for the Domitianic date is suggested by Revelation 6:5–6, which appears to be an allusion to an edict of Domitian. Revelation 6:5–6 says,

And when he broke the third seal, I heard the third living creature saying, "Come." And I looked, and behold, a black horse; and he who sat on it had a pair of scales in his hand. And I heard as it were a voice in the center of the four living creatures saying, "A quart of wheat for a denarius, and three quarts of barley for a denarius; and do not harm the oil and the wine."

In AD 92, in the face of a grain shortage, Domitian handed down a vine edict. In this edict he restricted provincial viticulture by ordering half of the vineyards of Asia Minor destroyed and no new ones planted to make room for growing more grain. Suetonius records the circumstances of the edict.

Once upon the occasion of a plentiful wine crop, attended with a scarcity of grain, thinking that the fields were neglected through too much attention to the vineyards, he made an edict forbidding anyone to plant more vines in Italy and ordering that the vineyards in the provinces be cut down, or but half of them at most be left standing; but he did not persist in carrying out the measure.[377]

The edict resulted in riots in Asia Minor because wine was a major source of income in that area. In response, Domitian revoked his earlier edict and ordered that anyone who allowed his vineyard to go out of production would be prosecuted. This event would have been a familiar, vivid allusion for John's readers of a case when grain was in shortage, but when it was illegal to harm the supply of oil and wine. It would have had particular applicability for the residents of

Philadelphia who were more dependent on viticulture than any city in Asia and whose volcanic soil was ideally suited for vines but not for corn.[378] Since Revelation 6:6 appears to be an intentional allusion to this event, Revelation had to be written after AD 92, thus, supporting the late date of Revelation.[379]

## John's Banishment to Patmos

Another internal argument for the AD 95 date of Revelation is the common practice of banishment to islands by Domitian. According to Revelation 1:10, when John wrote Revelation he was banished to the island of Patmos. While Nero did practice banishment, Domitian took it to another level, according to Dio Cassius and Suetonius. Nero had Paul and Peter executed in about AD 67–68. Under his rule the penalty for following Christ was death, but John was banished. Why the difference? If Revelation was written in AD 65, why wasn't John executed like Paul and Peter? The answer is clear—because he was banished under Domitian in AD 95, not by Nero in AD 65.

Additionally, there is no evidence that Nero ever banished a Christian as a Christian. However, according to Eusebius, Domitian banished a woman named Domitilla to an island named Pontia in AD 95 for being a Christian.[380] This parallels John's banishment to the island of Patmos in the very same year and provides more evidence that John was banished to the island of Patmos in AD 95 when he received the apocalyptic vision.

## The Martyrdom of Antipas

Revelation 2:13 mentions the martyrdom of a man

named Antipas in the city of Pergamum. According the church history, Antipas was martyred during the reign of Domitian in either AD 83 or 92.[381] Since the martyrdom of Antipas is in the past when Revelation was written, Revelation could not have been written before the reign of Domitian began in AD 81.

## Conclusion

While Hanegraaff's system has other weaknesses, the Achilles heel of his view is the date of Revelation. The evidence for the AD 95 date of Revelation is overwhelming. Yet, in spite of the overwhelming evidence in favor of the AD 95 date, and the fact that it is the dominant, traditional view of the church all the way back to the second century, Hanegraaff calls it "patently untenable." This statement is not surprising since his entire eschatological system depends on a mid-sixties date of Revelation, but it is shocking.

It is very unwise to construct one's entire eschatological framework on the foundation of the early date of Revelation, which at the very best is strongly disputed. Why would anyone adopt a view that is totally dependent on such a shaky foundation—especially when the AD 95 date is the view of the vast majority of scholars past and present? This would have to bother any preterist who objectively evaluates the evidence. We urge Hanegraaff to rethink his position and adopt an approach to eschatology in general and Revelation in particular that is not totally dependent upon the sandy foundation of a mid-sixties date for Revelation.

# AFTERWORD

Hank Hanegraaff in *The Apocalypse Code* desires to display an exegetical method that correctly interprets biblical prophecy for all its worth. We believe that he not only has failed in his objective, but his "exegetical eschatology" is a detriment to anyone desiring to find out what the Bible really teaches about prophecy. *AC* is primarily the recycling of failed hermeneutical principles from the past that have been demonstrated to provide a roadblock in one's effort to arrive at what Scripture intends to say. Even though the literal or historical-grammatical, contextual hermeneutic is referenced in Hanegraaff's method, it is clear that the bulk of his interpretive principles favor an allegorical approach and discredit the proper literal tradition. Repeatedly throughout *AC*, the clear meanings of passages are jettisoned in favor of fanciful speculation. Hanegraaff has desired to produce an "exegetical eschatology" or $(e^2)$," but the sad truth is that he has given us a model of "eisegetical eschatology"[382] or "e minus squared $(e\text{-}^2)$." If Hanegraaff's approach is followed, it will wreak havoc when applied, since the plain meaning of a text is no longer the basis for determining truth. Instead, the new authority becomes the imagination of the interpreter. This is not progress, but retrogression!

Since Hanegraaff's method is a hodge-podge of disconnected principles, it is not surprising to find that his method applied produces a potpourri theological outcome. Even though he readily labels the views of those with whom he interacts, Hanegraaff consistently resists labeling of his own views. He insists "that above all I am deeply committed to a proper *method* of biblical interpretation rather than to any particular *model* of eschatology."[383] Such a position is tenable in theory only, because the moment one applies a method, it then produces a model or outcome, whether he likes it or not. *AC* is a book that applies Hanegraaff's method. Therefore, outcomes about his model can be determined. It would be irrational to think one should or could avoid classification.

When analyzing the interpretive outcomes of *AC*, one is able to classify Hanegraaff's views into the following historical eschatological categories:

- He advocates a non-literal or allegorical hermeneutic.

- He is amillennial since he clearly rejects premillennialism and appears to lack the optimism of postmillennialism.

- His view of the timing of prophetic fulfillments is a blend of preterism and idealism, since he takes a partial preterist interpretation of some passages while interpreting other passages in an idealist manner.

- He clearly advocates replacement theology or supersessionism in relation to a future for national or ethnic Israel.

It is disappointing to think of the tremendous opportunity that Hanegraaff had to produce something in *AC* that would edify the church in the area of eschatology, only to realize that his book actually does damage. Therefore we must warn our readers about the dangers of this book and recommend that they reject Hanegraaff's method and its resulting model.

# WORKS CITED

## CHAPTER ONE

1. Hank Hanegraaff, *The Apocalypse Code* (Nashville: Thomas Nelson, 2007), 17.

2. Hanegraaff, *The Apocalypse Code*, 47.

3. Hanegraaff strangely says that Darby came up with the pre-trib rapture in 1831 and provides no support for that date. How does he know this? He also says that Darby invented "the concept of the secret [rapture] coming . . . " *The Apocalypse Code*, 45. Does he make this up out of thin air or is he just repeating old wives tales that he has heard? Hanegraaff is the first we have heard say that 1831 is the year Darby first thought of a pre-trib rapture.

4. Norman L. Geisler, "Review of Hank Hanegraaff's *The Apocalypse Code*," www.ses.edu/NormGeisler/ReviewApocalypseCode.html.

5. Charles C. Ryrie, *Dispensationalism* (Chicago: Moody Press, 1995), 15-16.

6. Geisler, "Review of Hank."

7. William E. Bell, "A Critical Evaluation of the Pretribulation Rapture Doctrine in Christian Eschatology" (Ph.D. diss., New York University, 1967), 26.

8. *The Shepherd of Hermas;* 1.4.2.

9. Paul J. Alexander, *The Byzantine Apocalyptic Tradition* (Berkeley: University of California Press, 1985), 136.

10. An English translation of the entire sermon can be found on the internet at the following: www.pre-trib.org/article-view.php?id=169.

11. Timothy J. Demy and Thomas D. Ice, "The Rapture and Pseudo-Ephraem: An Early Medieval Citation," *Bibliotheca Sacra* 152 (July–September 1995), 12.

12. Scholar Jonathan David Burnham said, "Until at least 1845 Darby taught that the rapture would occur three-and-a-half years before the second coming. He connected the rapture with the casting out of Satan from heaven in Revelation 12, an event he believed triggered the 'great tribulation' period." Burnham, "The Controversial Relationship Between Benjamin Wills Newton and John Nelson Darby" (Ph.D. diss., Oxford University, 1999), 128, f.n. 126.

13. Hanegraaff, *The Apocalypse Code*, 57.

14. Geisler, "Review of Hank." For a summary of the evidence for premillennialism in the early church see Norman Geisler, *Systematic Theology*, 4 vols. (Minneapolis: Bethany House Publishers, 2005), vol. 4, 567–71.

15. Geisler, *Systematic Theology*, vol. 4, 548–49.

16. See George Eldon Ladd, who Hanegraaff extols, in *The Blessed Hope: A Biblical Study of the Second Advent and the Rapture* (Grand Rapids: Eerdmans, 1956), 35ff.

17. See Thomas Ice, "The History of Preterism," in Tim LaHaye and Thomas Ice, editors, *The End Times Controversy: The Second Coming Under Attack* (Eugene, OR: Harvest House Publishers, 2003), 37-66.

18. Francis Gumerlock, "A Rapture Citation in the Fourteenth Century," *Bibliotheca Sacra* 159 (July—September 2002), 354-55.

19. Gumerlock, "A Rapture Citation," 356-59.

20. Gumerlock, "A Rapture Citation," 361.

21. Paul Boyer, *When Time Shall Be No More: Prophecy Belief in Modern American Culture* (Cambridge, MA: Belknap Press, 1992), 75.

22. Paul N. Benware, *Understanding End Times Prophecy: A Comprehensive Approach* (Chicago: Moody Press, 1995), 197-98.

23. Frank Marotta, *Morgan Edwards: An Eighteenth Century Pretribulationist* (Morganville, N.J.: Present Truth Publishers, 1995), 10-12.

24. The entire title of Asgill's work is as follows: *An Argument Proving, that According to the Covenant of Eternal Life Revealed in the Scriptures, Man may be Translated from Hence into that Eternal Life, without Passing through Death, although the Human Nature of Christ Himself could not be thus Translated till He had Passed Through Death.*

25. William Bramley-Moore, *The Church's Forgotten Hope or, Scriptural Studies on the Translation of the Saints* (Glasgow: Hobbs & Co., 1905), 322.

26. Morgan Edwards, *Two Academical Exercises on Subjects Bearing the following Titles; Millennium, Last-Novelties* (Philadelphia: Self-published, 1788). This entire book is available on the internet at the following: www.pre-trib.org/article-view.php?id=178.

27. Burnham, "The Controversial Relationship," 129.

28. Tim LaHaye and Jerry B. Jenkins, *Are We Living in the End Times? Current Events Foretold in Scripture ... And What They Mean* (Wheaton, IL: Tyndale House Publishers, 1999), 112-13.

29. Timothy C. F. Stunt, "Influences in the Early Development of J. N. Darby," in *Prisoners of Hope: Aspects of Evangelical Millennialism* in Britain and Ireland, 1800–1880 ed., Crawford Gribben and Timothy C. F. Stunt, editors, (Carlisle, UK: Paternoster Press, 2004), 64.

30. Crawford Gribben, *Rapture Fiction and The Evangelical* Crisis (Darlington, UK: Evangelical Press, 2006), 36.

31. Geisler, "Review of Hank."

32. David Bivin, "Perspective on the Caiaphas Tomb," Jerusalem Perspective Online, January 1, 2004.

33. Josephus, *Antiquities* 18.2.2; 18.4.3.

34. I (Mark) was unable to find one mainstream commentary on Matthew that adopts Hanegraaff's view of Matthew 26:63-66. Here are some of the commentaries that hold to the traditional view of this text. David L. Turner, The Gospel of Matthew, Cornerstone Biblical Commentary, vol. 11 (Carol Stream, IL: Tyndale, 2005), 348; John MacArthur, Jr. *Matthew 24-28* (Chicago: Moody, 1989), 207-8; D. A. Carson, "Matthew," in *The Expositor's Bible Commentary*, ed. Frank E. Gaebelein, vol. 8 (Grand Rapids: Zondervan, 1984), 555; Leon Morris, *The Gospel According to Matthew* (Grand Rapids: Eerdmans, 1992), 685; William Hendriksen, *The Gospel of Matthew*, New Testament Commentary (Grand Rapids: Baker, 1973), 932-33; Robert H. Mounce, Matthew, New International Biblical Commentary, ed. W. Ward Gasque (Peabody, MA: Hendrickson Publishers, 1991), 247.

35. Hanegraaff, *The Apocalypse Code*, 236.

36. Hanegraaff, *The Apocalypse Code*, 111.

37. Guthrie, *Introduction*, 950. The church of Smyrna probably did not exist during the time of Paul's ministry (Polycarp, *Letter to the Philippians* 11.3). Yet, in Revelation 2:9 the church had been suffering for some time. This is further support for the late date of Revelation.

38. Leon Morris, *Book of Revelation: An Introduction and Commentary* (Grand Rapids: Eerdmans, 1987), 37; Raymond E. Brown, *An Introduction to the New Testament*, Anchor Bible Reference Library, ed. David Noel Freedman (New York: Doubleday, 1997), 805; Ben Witherington III, *Revelation*, New Cambridge Bible Commentary, ed. Ben Witherington III (Cambridge: Cambridge University Press, 2003), 4; Vern S. Poythress, *The Returning King: A Guide to the Book of Revelation* (Phillipsburg, NJ: P & R Publishing, 2000), 50; Beale, *Revelation*, 12; Osborne, *Revelation*, 8.

39. We know from the letter of Pliny to the Emperor Trajan and from Trajan's response back to Pliny that believers were martyred for their faith in the early AD 90s in Asia's neighboring province, Bithynia (Pliny *Letters* 10.96–97). Pliny's letter provides hard evidence that at least in Asia's neighboring northern province there was persecution in the later years of Domitian's reign that led some believers to renounce their confession of faith in Christ.

40. Kenneth L. Gentry, Jr., *Before Jerusalem Fell* (Powder Springs, GA: American Vision, 1998), 298.

41. Guthrie, *Introduction*, 952.

42. Arnold Fruchtenbaum, *The Footsteps of the Messiah: A Study of the Sequence of Prophetic Events*, revised (Tustin, CA: Ariel Ministries Press, 2003), 577–93.

43. Fruchtenbaum, *Footsteps*, 593.

44. Some of the Old Testament passages that teach a future for Israel in her land include the following: Isa. 60:18, 21; Jer. 23:6–6; 24:5–6; 30:18; 31:31–34; 32:37–40; 33:6–9; Ezek. 28:25–26; 34:11–12; 36:24–26; 37:1–14, 21–25; 39:28; Hosea 3:4–5; Joel 2:18–29; Micah 2:12; 4:6–7; Zeph. 3:19–20; Zech. 8:7–8; 10:6–12; 13:8–9, etc.

45. Hanegraaff, *The Apocalypse Code*, 124.

46. Hanegraaff, *The Apocalypse Code*, 123.

47. Hanegraaff, *The Apocalypse Code*, 124.

48. Hanegraaff, *The Apocalypse Code*, 124.

49. Fruchtenbaum, *Footsteps*, 593.

50. Fruchtenbaum, *Footsteps*, 593–98.

51. Fruchtenbaum, *Footsteps*, 598.

52. Hanegraaff, *The Apocalypse Code*, 126

53. Edwin Yamauchi, "Ezra, Nehemiah," in *The Expositor's Bible Commentary*, ed. Frank E. Gaebelein, vol. 4 (Grand Rapids: Zondervan, 1988), 606.

54. Geisler, "Review of Hank."

55. Hanegraaff, *The Apocalypse Code*, 183

56. Blanche E. C. Dugdale, *Arthur James Balfour: First Earl of Balfour, 1848–1906* (New York: G. P. Putnam's Sons, 1937), 324.

57. Barbara W. Tuchman, *Bible and Sword: England and Palestine from the Bronze Age to Balfour* (New York: Ballatine Press, 1956), 311.

58. Tuchman, *Bible and Sword*, 83.

59. Tuchman, *Bible and Sword*, 312.

60. For an overview of the history of Christian Zionism see Thomas Ice, "Lovers of Zion: A History of Christian Zionism" at the following internet site: www.pre-trib.org/article-view.php?id=295.

61. Hanegraaff, *The Apocalypse Code*, xxii.

62. John Nelson Darby, *The Hopes of the Church of God, in Connection with the Destiny of the Jews and the Nations as Revealed in Prophecy* (1840), Collected Writings, vol. 2 (Winschoten, Netherlands: H. L. Heijkoop, reprint 1971), 324.

63. David A. Rausch, *Zionism Within Early American Fundamentalism 1878–1918: A Convergence of Two Traditions* (New York: The Edwin Mellen Press, 1979), 64.

64. David A. Rausch, "Evangelical Protestant Americans," in Moshe Davis, editor, *With Eyes Toward Zion–Volume II. Themes and Sources in the Archives of the United States, Great Britain, Turkey and Israel* (New York: Praeger, 1986), 324.

65. Hanegraaff, *The Apocalypse Code*, xxvii.

66. Hanegraaff, *The Apocalypse Code*, 2. Italics original.

## CHAPTER TWO

67. Hanegraaff, *The Apocalypse Code*, 3.

68. Hanegraaff, *The Apocalypse Code*, 3–10.

69. Hanegraaff, *The Apocalypse Code*, 2. Italics original.

70. Hanegraaff, *The Apocalypse Code*, 3.

71. Charles C. Ryrie, *Dispensationalism* (Chicago: Moody Press, [1966], 1995), 80–81.

72. Hanegraaff, *The Apocalypse Code*, 21. Hanegraaff characterizes LaHaye's interpretive approach as "a commonsense reading of Scripture" (17), "LaHaye's literalistic approach" (20), "hyper-literalism" (20), "a literalistic method of interpretation" (21), "a literal-at-all-costs method of interpretation" (21), "a woodenly literal sense" (21), and "a literalistic fashion" (34).

73. Hanegraaff, *The Apocalypse Code*, 32–35.

74. Hanegraaff, *The Apocalypse Code*, 32.

75. Hanegraaff, *The Apocalypse Code*, 33.

76. Hanegraaff, *The Apocalypse Code*, 23.

77. Hanegraaff, *The Apocalypse Code*, 32.

78. Robert L. Thomas, *Revelation 8–22: An Exegetical Commentary* (Chicago: Moody Press, 1995), 156.

79. In fact G. K. Beale wrote his Ph.D. dissertation on the use of Daniel in Revelation. See *The Use of Daniel in Jewish Apocalyptic Literature and in The Revelation of St. John* (Lanham, MD: University Press of America, 1984).

80. G. K. Beale, *The Book of Revelation: A Commentary on the Greek Text* (Grand Rapids: Eerdmans, 1999), 683.

81. Beale, *Revelation*, 685.

82. Hanegraaff, *The Apocalypse Code*, 144–52. For a refutation of Hanegraaff's view see Andy Woods, "Revelation 13 and the First Beast," in Tim LaHaye and Thomas Ice, editors, *The End Times Controversy: The Second Coming Under Attack* (Eugene, OR: Harvest House Publishers, 2003), 237–50.

83. Bernard Ramm, *Protestant Biblical Interpretation: A Textbook of Hermeneutics*, 3rd edition, (Grand Rapids: Baker Book House, 1970), 58.

84. For futurist answers to many of Hanegraaff's preterist views see Tim LaHaye and Thomas Ice, editors, *The End Times Controversy: The Second Coming Under Attack* (Eugene, OR: Harvest House Publishers, 2003), and Thomas Ice and Kenneth L. Gentry, Jr., *The Great Tribulation: Past or Future?* (Grand Rapids: Kregel Publications, 1999).

85. Hanegraaff, *The Apocalypse Code*, 9.

86. Hanegraaff, *The Apocalypse Code*, 172.

87. Roy B. Zuck, *Basic Bible Interpretation: A Practical Guide to Discovering Biblical Truth* (Wheaton, IL.: Victor Books, 1991), 176.

88. Hanegraaff, *The Apocalypse Code*, 9.

89. Hanegraaff, *The Apocalypse Code*, 170.

90. The Book of Revelation says that the 144,000 believers are "sealed" by the Lord, not "marked" as is said of the Beast's imprint.

91. Hanegraaff, *The Apocalypse Code*, 174.

92. Hanegraaff, *The Apocalypse Code*, 174.

93. Hanegraaff, *The Apocalypse Code*, 182.

94. Geisler, "Review of Hank."

95. A term coined by British scholar Paul Wilkinson of those who reject biblical Zionism and champion the Palestinian cause against Israel. Paul Richard Wilkinson, "John Nelson Darby and the Origins of Christian Zionism" (Ph.D. thesis, Univ. of Manchester, 2006), 88–121.

96. Hanegraaff, *The Apocalypse Code*, 9.

97. Hanegraaff, *The Apocalypse Code*, 230.

98. Zuck, *Basic Bible Interpretation*, 39.

99. Ramm, *Protestant Biblical Interpretation*, 55.

100. John Calvin as cited in Frederic W. Farrar, *History of Interpretation* (Grand Rapids: Baker Book House, [1886] 1961), 347.

101. Ramm, *Protestant Biblical Interpretation*, 59.

102. Hanegraaff, *The Apocalypse Code*, 3.

103. Hanegraaff's reluctance to be known as a preterist may come from his misunderstanding the use of the term down through church history. Historically a preterist was originally a partial or mild preterist. Full or hyper-preterism did not develop until the nineteenth century and was the last of the three types of preterism (i.e., mild, moderate and full) to develop. (For a more extensive description of preterism see Thomas Ice, *What is Preterism?* in Tim LaHaye & Thomas Ice, editors, *The End Times Controversy: The Second Coming Under Attack* [Eugene, OR: Harvest House Publishers, 2003], 17–35.) Historically a preterist is one who saw at least part of Revelation fulfilled in the destruction of Jerusalem in AD 70. Such an understanding is clearly Hanegraaff's view. Since Hanegraaff takes preterist interpretations of the book of Revelation, it makes him

a preterist. (For more on the history of preterism see Thomas Ice, "The History of Preterism," in LaHaye & Ice, *End Times Controversy*, 37–66.)

104. Hal Lindsey, *The Late Great Planet Earth* (Grand Rapids: Zondervan, 1970).

105. Hanegraaff, *The Apocalypse Code*, 1. Italics original.

106. BDAG or Frederick William Danker and Walter Bauer, *A Greek-English Lexicon of the New Testament and Other Early Christian Literature*, a translation and adaptation by William F. Arndt & F. Wilbur Gingrich (Chicago: The University of Chicago Press, 2000), 349.

107. BDAG, 349.

108. Walter C. Kaiser, Jr., "A Response to Author's Intention and Biblical Interpretation" in Earl D. Radmacher and Robert D. Preus, editors, *Hermeneutics, Inerrancy, & the Bible* (Grand Rapids: Zondervan, 1984), 442.

## CHAPTER THREE

109. David L. Cooper, *The World's Greatest Library: Graphically Illustrated* (Los Angeles: Biblical Research Society, 1970), 11.

110. Tim LaHaye and Jerry B. Jenkins, *Are We Living in the End Times? Current Events Foretold in Scripture . . . And What They Mean* (Wheaton, IL: Tyndale House Publishers, 1999), 6.

111. *Webster's New Twentieth Century Dictionary*, Unabridged, Second Edition, 1055.

112. *The Compact Edition of The Oxford English Dictionary* (New York, Oxford Press, 1971), s.v., "literal."

113. Paul Lee Tan, *The Interpretation of Prophecy*, (Winona Lake, Ind.: Assurance Publishers, 1974), 29.

114. Bernard Ramm, *Protestant Biblical Interpretation: A Textbook of Hermeneutics*, 3rd. edition (Grand Rapids: Baker Book House), 1970), 119.

115. This is essentially the interpretation given by John Calvin in his commentary. John Calvin, *Commentary on the Book of the Prophet Isaiah*, Vol. 1, translated from the original Latin, by the Rev. William Pringle (Grand Rapids: Baker Book House, 1979), 89-103.

116. *Tim LaHaye Prophecy Study Bible*, KJV (Chattanooga, TN: AMG Publishers, 2000), 691.

117. Charles C. Ryrie, *Dispensationalism* (Chicago: Moody Press, [1966], 1995), 80.

118. Roy B. Zuck, *Basic Bible Interpretation: A Practical Guide to Discovering Biblical Truth* (Wheaton, Ill.: Victor Books, 1991), 100.

119. Zuck, *Basic Bible Interpretation*, 100-01.

120. Tan, *Interpretation of Prophecy*, 103.

121. Zuck, *Basic Bible Interpretation*, 77.

122. Ryrie, *Dispensationalism*, 80-81.

123. Hanegraaff, *The Apocalypse Code*, 124–25.

124. Elliott E. Johnson, *Expository Hermeneutics: An Introduction* (Grand Rapids: Zondervan, 1990), 9.

125. Ramm, *Protestant Biblical Interpretation*, 126.

126. Floyd E. Hamilton, *The Basis of Millennial Faith* (Grand Rapids: Eerdmans, 1942), 38.

127. Oswald T. Allis, *Prophecy and the Church* (Phillipsburg, NJ: Presbyterian and Reformed Publishing, [1945] 1947), 238.

128. Tan, *Interpretation of Prophecy*, 63.

129. Ryrie, *Dispensationalism*, 81.

130. Arnold Fruchtenbaum, *The Footsteps of the Messiah: A Study of the Sequence of Prophetic Events*, revised (Tustin, CA: Ariel Ministries Press, 2003), 801–08.

131. John F. Walvoord, *The Revelation of Jesus Christ: A Commentary* (Chicago: Moody Press, 1966), 29–30.

132. Walvoord, *Revelation*, 29–30.

133. John F. Walvoord, *Prophecy: 14 Essential Keys to Understanding the Final Drama* (Nashville: Thomas Nelson Publisher, 1993), 11.

## CHAPTER FOUR

134. For example Proverbs 5:4, 11; 14:12, 13; 16:25; 18:18; 20:21; 25:8; 29:21.

135. Bernard Ramm, *Protestant Biblical Interpretation: A Textbook of Hermeneutics*, 3rd edition, (Grand Rapids: Baker Book House, 1970), 49.

136. Joseph W. Trigg, "Introduction," in R. P. C. Hanson, *Allegory & Event: A Study of the Sources and Significance of Origen's Interpretation of Scripture* (Louisville: Westminster John Knox Press, 2002), vi.

137. Ronald E. Diprose, *Israel in the development of Christian thought* (Rome: Instituto Biblico Evangelico Italiano, 2000), 87. Frederic W.

Farrar explains further: "The Bible, he [Origen] argued, is meant for the salvation of man; but man, as Plato tells us, consists of three parts—body, soul, and spirit. Scripture therefore must have a threefold sense corresponding to this trichotomy. It has a literal, a moral, and a mystic meaning analogous to the body, to the soul, to the spirit .... But of two of these three supposed senses Origen makes very little use. To the moral sense he refers but seldom; to the literal sense scarcely at all." Frederic W. Farrar, *History of Interpretation* (Grand Rapids: Baker Book House, [1886] 1961), 196–97.

138. Diprose, *Israel*, 87–88.

139. Hanegraaff, *The Apocalypse Code*, 21.

140. Hanegraaff, *The Apocalypse Code*, 23.

141. Hanegraaff, *The Apocalypse Code*, 22.

142. Hanegraaff, *The Apocalypse Code*, 23.

143. Ramm, *Protestant Biblical Interpretation*, 49.

144. R. H. Charles, *Studies in the Apocalypse* (Edinburgh: T & T Clark, 1913), 11.

145. Diprose, *Israel*, 89. (emphasis original)

146. See for example, Hanegraaff, *Apocalypse Code*, 116, 124, 127, 180, 199, 200, 221.

147. Diprose, *Israel*, 90.

148. Hanegraaff, *The Apocalypse Code*, 115–16, 117–24, 233–35.

149. Hanegraaff, *The Apocalypse Code*, 116, 124–28, 135–36.

150. Hank Hanegraaff, "Response to *National Liberty Journal* article on *The Apocalypse Code*, www.equip.org/site/apps/nl/content2.asp?c=muI1 LaMNJrE&b=2616123&ct=3839317.

151. Geisler, "Review of Hank." It is interesting that Hanegraaff does understand his own model within a historical context of what the church has believed throughout her history. Thinking that he does not hold to any form of replacement theology he says, "God has only ever had one chosen people who form one covenant community, . . . As such, the true church is true Israel, and true Israel is truly the church—one cannot replace what it already is." Hanegraaff, "Response."

152. Henry Preserved Smith, *Essays in Biblical Interpretation* (Boston: Marshall Jones Company, 1921), 58.

153. Farrar, *History of Interpretation*, 245–46.

154. Ramm, *Protestant Biblical Interpretation*, 51.

155. Ramm, *Protestant Biblical Interpretation*, 52.

156. Martin Luther cited in Ramm, *Protestant Biblical Interpretation*, 54.

157. John Calvin cited in Ramm, *Protestant Biblical Interpretation*, 58.

158. Jeffrey K. Jue documents how Joseph Mede and a host of many others among the English began adopting a millennialist view of eschatology. Jue says, "By the mid-seventeenth century the most popular eschatological position in England was millenarianism." *Heaven Upon Earth: Joseph Mede (1586–1638) and the Legacy of Millenarianism* (Dordrecht, Holland: Springer, 2006), 4.

159. Jue notes that, "the majority of New England puritans held to the doctrine of a future national conversion of ethnic Jews." *Heaven Upon Earth*, 191. "The doctrine of the national conversion of the Jews was an integral part of the eschatology of the New England settlers." Jue, *Heaven Upon Earth*, 193. "Virtually all seventeenth- and early eighteenth-century millennialists on both sides of the Atlantic agreed that even though the Jews were still languishing in their Diaspora, Jehovah had not forgotten his chosen people and would, in due time, restore them to their once-elevated position among the nations." Reiner Smolinski, *The Threefold Paradise of Cotton Mather: An Edition of "Triparadisus,"* (Athens, GA: The University of Georgia Press, 1995), 21.

160. Wallis tells us: "The rediscovery of the last five chapters of Irenaeus about 1570 may have contributed to Alsted's formulation of premillennialism, since he and others used the writers of the ancient church. We may feel that the intensive Bible study of the Reformation, combined with the knowledge of antiquity, was beginning to swing the pendulum back to the primitive premillennialism of Irenaeus which had been rejected by Augustine." Wilber B. Wallis, "Reflections on the History of Premillennial Thought," in R. Laird Harris, Swee-Hwa Quek, & J. Robert Vannoy, editors, *Interpretation & History: Essays in honour of Allen A. MacRae* (Singapore: Christian Life Publishers, 1986), 229. Early Puritan Joseph "Mede observed a similarity between Patristic chiliasm and his own millenarianism especially the writings of the Ante-Nicene fathers. However, in the early sixteenth century any appeal to the Ante-Nicene fathers' views on the Apocalypse was discouraged for fear of encouraging their chiliasm." Jue, *Heaven Upon Earth*, 110.

161. In a note on Romans 11:25, The Geneva Bible says, "The blindness of the Jews is neither so universal that the Lord hath no elect in that nation, neither shall it be continual for there shall be a time wherein they also (as the Prophets have forewarned) shall effectually embrace that which they do now so stubbornly for the most part reject and refuse." *The 1599 Geneva Bible* (White Hall, WV: Tolle Lege Press, 2006), 1155. Notice that this note believes that the Old Testament Prophets also taught a future for Israel as well.

162. Jue, *Heaven Upon Earth*, 199.

163. Bernard Ramm has entitled his presentation of literal interpretation or the historical, grammatical, and contextual method as Protestant Biblical Interpretation in his book with that title. Bernard Ramm, *Protestant Biblical Interpretation: A Textbook of Hermeneutics*, 3rd edition, (Grand Rapids: Baker Book House, 1970).

164. Wallis, "Reflections," 229.

165. Wallis, "Reflections," 232–34.

166. Wallis, "Reflections," 234.

167. Beryl Smalley, *The Study of the Bible in the Middle Ages* (Notre Dame, IN: University of Notre Dame Press, [1964], 1982), 358.

168. Smalley, *The Study*, 359.

169. Smalley, *The Study*, 360. Traditionally non-literal interpretation has been an old garment that has been labeled "spiritualizing." In this approach the words of the author are clothed with some deeper spiritual sense. With this method of interpretation, the words of the Old Testament prophets are often explained away. A more recent and "fashionable" term is *sensus plenior*. Use of this concept involves finding a "fuller meaning" that the author did not clearly intend. The "layered look" is also finding its way into the evangelical community as some are returning to the multiple meanings of the text once held by the Schoolmen of the Middle Ages. Waltke suggests a fourfold approach: historical, typical, anagogical, and moral. See Bruce K. Waltke, "The Schoolmen's Hermeneutics Reconsidered," an unpublished paper given at the Northwest Evangelical Theological meeting: April 1993.

170. "An Interview: Dr. John F. Walvoord Looks at Dallas Seminary," *Dallas Connection* (Winter 1994, Vol. 1, No. 3), 4.

171. Walter C. Kaiser, Jr., "Evangelical Hermeneutics: Restatement, Advance or Retreat from the Reformation?" *Concordia Theological*

*Quarterly* 46 (1982), 167. Kaiser believes that the present-day crisis finds its historical roots in the writings of liberal existentialists like Friedrich Schleirmacher (1768-1834), Wilhelm Dilthey (1833-1911), Martin Heidegger (1889-1976), Rudolf Bultmann (1884-1976), and Hans Georg Gadamer (b. 1900). Kaiser, "Evangelical Hermeneutics," 167.

172. Kaiser, "Evangelical Hermeneutics," 167.

173. Kaiser, "Evangelical Hermeneutics," 167.

174. Geisler, "Review of Hank."

175. Hanegraaff, *The Apocalypse Code*, 2.

176. Geisler, "Review of Hank."

## CHAPTER FIVE

177. Tim LaHaye and Jerry B. Jenkins, *The Indwelling: The Beast Takes Possession* (Wheaton: Tyndale, 2000), 366-67.

178. Hank Hanegraaff, *The Apocalypse Code: Find Out What the Bible Really Says About The End Times and Why It Matters Today* (Nashville: Thomas Nelson, 2007), xix–xx.

179. Hank Hanegraaff and Sigmund Brouwer, *The Last Disciple* (Wheaton: Tyndale, 2004), 394.

180. Tim LaHaye, *Revelation Illustrated and Made Plain* (Grand Rapids: Zondervan, 1973, 1975), 180.

181. LaHaye, *Revelation*, 180.

182. Hanegraaff and Brouwer, *The Last Disciple*, 395.

183. Hanegraaff and Brouwer, *The Last Disciple*, 395.

184. Gregory H. Harris, "Satan's Deceptive Miracles in the Tribulation," *Bibliotheca Sacra* (July–Sept. 1999; vol. 156, no. 623), 317.

185. Hanegraaff and Brouwer, *The Last Disciple*, 394. (Italics original).

186. Harris, "Satan's Deceptive Miracles," 313. Gregory Harris has done a great deal of work on these matters and strongly concludes that these things are true miracles and not just magic tricks. See also Gregory H. Harris, "Satan's Work as a Deceiver," *Bibliotheca Sacra* (April–June 1999; vol. 156, no. 622), 190–202; "The Wound of the Beast in the Tribulation," *Bibliotheca Sacra* (Oct.–Dec. 1999; vol. 156, no. 624), 459–468; "The Theme of Deception During the Tribulation," Th.D Dissertation, 1998, Dallas Theological Seminary.

187.  William F. Arndt and F. W. Gingrich, *A Greek-English Lexicon of the New Testament* (Chicago: University of Chicago Press, 1957), 755.

188.  George Abbott-Smith, *A Manual Greek Lexicon of the New Testament*, 3rd edition (Edinburgh: T & T Clark, 1937), 443.

189.  Joseph Henry Thayer, *A Greek-English Lexicon of the New Testament* (New York: American Book Company, 1889), 620.

190.  Harris, "Satan's Deceptive Miracles," 310.

191.  Harris, "Satan's Deceptive Miracles," 310.

192.  Philip Edgcumbe Hughes, *A Commentary on the Epistle to the Hebrews* (Grand Rapids: Eerdmans, 1977), 80–81.

193.  Harris, "Satan's Deceptive Miracles," 311.

194.  Harris, "Satan's Deceptive Miracles," 311.

195.  Harris, "Satan's Deceptive Miracles," 311.

196.  The book of Job tells us that God allowed Satan to cause fire to fall from the sky and destroy people and sheep (Job 1:16). God even allowed Satan to bring a great wind that blew down a building (Job 1:19).

197.  John F. Walvoord, "Revelation," in *The Bible Knowledge Commentary, New Testament*, ed. John F. Walvoord and Roy B. Zuck (Wheaton, IL: Victor, 1983), 961.

198.  Gregory H. Harris, "The Wound of the Beast in the Tribulation," *Bibliotheca Sacra* (Oct.–Dec. 1999; vol. 156, no. 624), 466. The argument that we present is primarily that made by Harris.

199.  Charles C. Ryrie, *Revelation*, Everyman's Bible Commentary (Chicago: Moody, 1968), 83.

200.  Leon Morris, *The Revelation of St. John*, Tyndale New Testament Commentaries (Grand Rapids: Eerdmans, 1969), 167.

201.  Harris, "Wound of the Beast," 467.

202.  Harris, "Wound of the Beast," 467.

203.  William Lee, "The Revelation of St. John," in *The Holy Bible* (London: John Murray, 1881), Vol. 4, 789.

204.  Hank Hanegraaff and Sigmund Brouwer, *The Last Disciple* (Wheaton: Tyndale, 2004), 394.

205.  Robert L. Thomas, "Exegetical Digest: Revelation 8–14" (n. p.: by the author, 1993), 280.

206. Harris, "Wound of the Beast," 469.

207. For specific details concerning documentation of these advocates see Harris, "Wound of the Beast," footnote 27. John MacArthur believes that Rev. 13 refers to the future Antichrist whose death and resurrection may be "real or fake." John MacArthur, *Revelation 12-22* (Chicago: Moody Press, 2000), 45-46. While MacArthur holds to the idea that the Beast's death and resurrection are counterfeit, he is open to the idea of a real death and resurrection.

## CHAPTER SIX

208. Hank Hanegraaff, *The Apocalypse Code* (Nashville: Thomas Nelson, 2007), 37–48, 69.

209. Hanegraaff, *The Apocalypse Code*, 40.

210. Hanegraaff, *The Apocalypse Code*, 41.

211. Ernest R. Sandeen, said, "Darby held an open mind . . . as late as 1843" in *The Roots of Fundamentalism: British and American Millenarianism, 1800–1930* (Grand Rapids: Baker Book House, 1970), 38. Darby scholar Jonathan David Burnham says that Darby's formulation of pre-tribulationism "did not feature prominently in his writings during the 1830s, . . . Darby wavered in his commitment to it until about 1843," in "The Controversial Relationship Between Benjamin Wills Newton and John Nelson Darby" (Ph.D. diss., Oxford University, 1999), 128.

212. Timothy C. F. Stunt, "Influences in the Early Development of J. N. Darby," in Crawford Gribben and Timothy C. F. Stunt, editors, *Prisoners of Hope: Aspects of Evangelical Millennialism in Britain and Ireland, 1800–1880* (Carlisle, UK: Paternoster Press, 2004), 60, f.n. 60. See also Stunt who says that Darby was mostly in Paris between 1829 and 1832 doing evangelism in Timothy C. F. Stunt, "John Nelson Darby: Contexts and Perceptions," in Crawford Gribben and Andrew R. Holmes, editors, *Protestant Millennialism, Evangelicalism and Irish Society, 1790–2005* (Hampshire, UK: Palgrave Macmillan, 2006), 85.

213. Norman L. Geisler, "Review of Hank Hanegraaff's *The Apocalypse Code*," www.ses.edu/NormGeisler/ReviewApocalypseCode.html.

214. J. N. Darby, *Letters*, 3 vols (London, n.d.), vol. 2, 254.

215. Geisler, "Review of Hank."

216. Hanegraaff, *The Apocalypse Code*, 173.

217. Ernest Best, *The International Critical Commentary, Ephesians* (Edinburgh: T & T Clark, 1998), 306.

218. Hanegraaff, *The Apocalypse Code*, 125.

219. Hanegraaff on more than one occasion compares LaHaye to the liberal and foul-mouthed Bill Maher in *The Apocalypse Code*, 13–15, 35. In another instance he opens a chapter by comparing LaHaye to Bill Clinton and his fiasco relating to what "is" is in *The Apocalypse Code*, 70–73.

220. Jehovah Witnesses, while premillennialists are not futurists like LaHaye and dispensationalists, instead they are historicists who believe in a single redeemed people of God throughout history. What is historicism? Historicism is one of the four major interpretive approaches that people take in relation to the book of Revelation and biblical prophecy in general. The four views are simple in the sense that they reflect the only four possible ways that one can relate to time, which are past, present, future, and timeless. When speaking of the fulfillment of Bible prophecy these four timing possibilities are called preterism (past), historicism (present), futurism (future), and idealism (timeless).

The *preterist* (Latin for "past" or "gone by") believes that most, if not all prophecy has already been fulfilled, usually in relation to the destruction of Jerusalem in AD 70. The *historicist* sees much of the current church age as equal to the tribulation period. Thus, in relation to our day, most prophecy has already been fulfilled and will be fulfilled during the current church age. *Futurists* usually believe that almost no prophetic events are occurring in the current church age, but will take place in the following future events: the seven-year tribulation, the second coming, the 1,000-year millennium, and the eternal state. The *idealist* does not believe either that the Bible indicates the timing of events or that we can determine their timing in advance. Therefore, idealists see prophetic passages as a teacher of great truths about God to be applied to our present lives.

Historicism, once the dominant view of Protestants from the Reformation until the middle of the nineteenth century, whether one was an amillennialist, postmillennialist, or premillennialist. Today, historicism exerts little attraction as a system of prophetic interpretation for evangelical Christians, who became tired of their endless and errant date-setting schemes. Three of the four major cults of the nineteenth century were developed when historicism was dominant, including the Seventh-Day Adventists, Mormons, and Jehovah Witnesses. To be a historicist virtually requires one to engage in date setting of the second coming. One cannot hold to historicism and a pre-trib rapture since they view most of the tribulation as taking place throughout much of the 2,000 years of church history. They turn the 2,300 days of Daniel 8 and the 1,260 days of Daniel and Revelation into years via their day/year scheme. The common historicist view is that the tribulation began with the rise of the Antichrist, which began when Constantine Christianized the Roman Empire in AD 313. Since that time, the seal, trumpet, and bowl judgments have for the most part already taken place and they are awaiting Armageddon and the second coming. This is why most expressions of historicism cannot believe in the two peoples of God, as do dispensational futurists (i.e., Israel and the church). Like Hanegraaff and not LaHaye, they see only a future for the church and not Israel. However, it must be noted that most historicists take a preterist view of parts of the Olivet Discourse, but disassociate it from the tribulation as found in Revelation and most New Testament Epistles.

221. Hanegraaff, *The Apocalypse Code*, 124–25.

222. Hanegraaff, *The Apocalypse Code*, 125.

223. Roy B. Zuck, *Basic Bible Interpretation: A Practical Guide to Discovering Biblical Truth* (Wheaton, IL: Victor Books, 1991). We highly recommend this book as a great source to ground anyone in the basic of interpreting the Bible, including Bible prophecy.

224. Zuck, *Basic Bible Interpretation*, 145.

225. E. W. Bullinger, *Figures of Speech Used in the Bible: Explained and Illustrated,* reprint (Grand Rapids: Baker book House, [1898] 1968).

226. Zuck, *Basic Bible Interpretation*, 143.

227. Bullinger, *Figures of Speech*, xv, cited in Zuck, *Basic Bible Interpretation*, 143.

228. Zuck, *Basic Bible Interpretation*, 146. The final three include: "4. Take the figurative sense if the literal would demand immoral action …. 5. Note whether a figurative expression is followed by an explanatory literal statement …. 6. Sometimes a figure is marked by a qualifying adjective, … "

229. Matthew Waymeyer, *Revelation 20 and the Millennial Debate* (The Woodlands, TX: Kress Christian Publications, 2004), 50 (emphasis original).

230. An allegorical interpretation is what it is. If an interpreter designates a word or phrase as a figure of speech when in that context such is not the case, then their interpretation would be an allegorical one. An

allegorical interpretation is where a person reads an idea from outside the text under consideration and imposes it on that text. Hanegraaff's belief that the 144,000 are a figurative designation for believers in general is not supported by the passage, thus, an allegorical interpretation.

231. Hanegraaff, *The Apocalypse Code*, 126.

232. Hanegraaff, *The Apocalypse Code*, 126.

233. Our suggestion is also the view of Robert L. Thomas, *Revelation 1–7: An Exegetical Commentary* (Chicago: Moody Press, 1992), 476–77, who says the following of the literal view of Israel: "This accounts for the detailed division of the people of God into twelve families answering individually to the twelve tribes of Israel in vv. 5–8, and is the explanation favored by the earliest Christian tradition."

234. Thomas, *Revelation 1–7*, 477.

235. Arnold G. Fruchtenbaum, *Israelology: The Missing Link in Systematic Theology*, revised (Tustin, CA: Ariel Ministries Press, 1993) is an expanded version of his Ph.D. dissertation from New York University.

236. This study is provided in Fruchtenbaum, *Israelology*, 684–99.

237. Fruchtenbaum, *Israelology*, 699 (emphasis original).

238. Thomas, *Revelation 1–7*, 476.

239. Nathaniel West, *The Thousand Years in Both Testaments*, reprint (Fincastle, VA: Scripture Truth Book Company [1889] n.d.), 92.

240. Geisler, "Review of Hank."

241. Hanegraaff, *The Apocalypse Code*, 126.

242. Zuck, *Basic Bible Interpretation*, 187.

243. Thomas, *Revelation 1–7*, 478.

244. Hanegraaff, *The Apocalypse Code*, 126.

245. Thomas, *Revelation 1–7*, 478.

246. Jeffrey Louie, "An Expositional Study of the 144,000 in The Book of The Revelation" (Ph.D. diss., Dallas Theological Seminary, 1990), 38.

247. Louie, "An Expositional Study of the 144,000," 39–40.

248. Louie, "An Expositional Study of the 144,000," 41.

249. Hanegraaff, *The Apocalypse Code*, 125 (emphasis original).

250. Hanegraaff, *The Apocalypse Code*, 125.

251. Thomas, *Revelation 1–7*, 482.

252. Thomas, *Revelation 1–7*, 484.

## CHAPTER SEVEN

253. Hank Hanegraaff, *The Apocalypse Code: Find Out What the Bible Really Says About The End Times and Why It Matters Today* (Nashville: Thomas Nelson, 2007), 224–25.

254. Michael J. Vlach, "The Church as a Replacement of Israel: An Analysis of Supersessionism," (Ph.D. dissertation at Southeaster Baptist Theological Seminary, Wake Forest, NC, 2004), xv. Hanegraaff uses the term "true Israel" for the church a number of times throughout *AC*. See for example the following use of "true Israel," 116, 124, 199, 200, and "spiritual Israel," 221.

255. "The term 'replacement theology' (cf. 'Christian supersessionism') is a relatively new term in Christian theology," says Ronald E. Diprose, *Israel in the development of Christian thought* (Rome: Instituto Biblico Evangelico Italiano, 2000), 31, f.n. 2.

256. Vlach, "Replacement of Israel," 10.

257. Hank Hanegraaff, "Response to *National Liberty Journal* article on *The Apocalypse Code*, www.equip.org/site/apps/nl/content2.asp?c=muI1 LaMNJrE&b=2616123&ct=3839317.

258. Hanegraaff, "Response."

259. Diprose, *Israel*, 3.

260. Diprose, *Israel*, 31. [emphasis original]

261. Hanegraaff calls the church the "true Israel" (116, 124, 127, 180, 199, 200) or "spiritual Israel" (221) a number of times in *AC*. In the acknowledgments section of the *AC*, Hanegraaff cites a list of individuals and expresses his "deep appreciation for the insights I garnered through such intellects as N. T. Wright, Gary Burge, Stephen Sizer, Colin Chapman, Timothy Weber, R. C. Sproul, Gary DeMar, Kenneth Gentry Jr., David Chilton, Steve Gregg, Dennis Johnson, Gene Edward Veith Jr., Gordon Fee, Keith Mathison, Richard Bauckham, and Gretchen Passantino." Hanegraaff, *Apocalypse Code*, xiii. Virtually all those cited are outspoken advocates of replacement theology, which Hanegraaff relies on and quotes in support of his views of Israel and the church. For example, Kenneth Gentry said: "We believe that the international church has superseded for all times **national** Israel as the **institution** for the administration of divine blessing to the world."

[emphasis original] Kenneth L. Gentry, Jr., "Supersessional Orthodoxy; Zionistic Sadism," *Dispensationalism in Transition*, Vol. VI, No. 2; Feb. 1993, 1. Colin Chapman does not state his views as clearly as Gentry, but nevertheless says, "the coming of the kingdom of God through Jesus the Messiah has transformed and reinterpreted all the promises and prophecies in the Old Testament .... Jesus the Messiah, who lived, died and was raised from death *in the land*, has opened the kingdom of God to people of all races, making all who follow Him into 'one new humanity' (Ephesians 2:15, NRSV)." [emphasis original] Colin Chapman, *Whose Promised Land? The Continuing Crisis Over Israel and Palestine* (Grand Rapids: Baker, 2002), 285.

262. Vlach, "Replacement of Israel," xvii.

263. Hanegraaff, *Apocalypse Code*, 124. His chapter on the typology principle (161–226) is full of instances where he reduces Old Testament prophecy to a type of the real fulfillment in the New Testament, most of them relating to how the church fulfills in the New what was promised to Israel in the Old.

264. Hanegraaff, *The Apocalypse Code*, 201.

265. Hanegraaff, *The Apocalypse Code*, 174.

266. Hanegraaff, *The Apocalypse Code*, 190.

267. Hanegraaff, *The Apocalypse Code*, 202–03.

268. Hanegraaff, *The Apocalypse Code*, 223.

269. Hanegraaff, *The Apocalypse Code*, 223.

270. Hanegraaff, *The Apocalypse Code*, 182.

271. Hanegraaff, *The Apocalypse Code*, 221.

272. Hanegraaff, *The Apocalypse Code*, 180.

273. See endnote number 9 for documentation.

274. Vlach, "Replacement of Israel," xvii.

275. Hanegraaff, *The Apocalypse Code*, 197.

276. Hanegraaff, *The Apocalypse Code*, 200.

277. Hanegraaff, *The Apocalypse Code*, 201.

278. Stephen Sizer, *Christian Zionists: Road-map to Armageddon?* (Leicester, England: Inter-Varsity Press, 2004), 182, as cited in Hanegraaff, *The Apocalypse Code*, 222.

279. Norman L. Geisler, "Review of Hank Hanegraaff's *The Apocalypse Code*," www.ses.edu/NormGeisler/ReviewApocalypseCode.html.

280. Passages include: Gen. 12:7; 13:14–15; 15:18; 17:8; Lev. 26:33, 43; Deut. 26:9; 30:1–11; Josh. 24:20–28; 2 Sam. 7:11–16; Ezra 4:1–3; Psalm 102:13–20; Isa. 11:11–12; 18:7; 27:12–13; 29:1, 8; 44; 60:8–21; 66:18–22; Jer. 3:17–18; 7:7; 11:10–11; 23:3–6; 25:5; 29:14; 30:7, 10; 31:2, 10, 23, 31–34; 33:4–16; 50:19; Ezek. 11:17; 20:33–37; 22:19–22; 28:25; 36:23–24, 38; 37:21–22; 39:28; Dan. 12:1; Hosea 3:4–5; Joel 3:20–21; Amos 9:9, 14–15; Micah 2:12; 3:9–10; 4:7, 11–12; Zeph. 2:1–3; Zech. 7:7–8; 8:1–8; 10:6–12; 12:2–10; 13:8–9; 14:1, 5, 9; Mal. 3:6.

281. Relevant passages include: Matt. 19:28; 23:37; Luke 21:24, 29–33, Acts 15:14–17; Rom. 11; Rev. 11:1–2; 12.

282. Walter C. Kaiser, Jr. "The Land of Israel and The Future Return (Zechariah 10:6–12)," in H. Wayne House, editor, *Israel: The Land and the People: An Evangelical Affirmation of God's Promises* (Grand Rapids, Kregel, 1998), 211.

283. Hanegraaff, *The Apocalypse Code*, 225.

284. Hanegraaff, *The Apocalypse Code*, 177.

285. John F. Walvoord, *Major Bible Prophecies: 37 Crucial Prophecies That Affect You Today* (Grand Rapids: Zondervan, 1991), 77.

286. Note the following references in Genesis: 12:1–3, 7–9; 13:14–18; 15:1–18; 17:1–27; 22:15–19; 26:2–6, 24–25; 27:28–29, 38–40; 28:1–4, 10–22; 31:3, 11–13; 32:22–32; 35:9–15; 48:3–4, 10–20; 49:1–28; 50:23–25.

287. Walvoord, *Major Bible Prophecies*, 77–78.

288. Walter C. Kaiser, Jr., *Toward an Old Testament Theology* (Grand Rapids: Zondervan, 1978), 124-25.

289. See Hanegraaff, *The Apocalypse Code*, 118–24.

290. See Hanegraaff, *The Apocalypse Code*, 124–28.

291. Walter C. Kaiser, Jr., "An Assessment of 'Replacement Theology,'" *Mishkan* (No. 21; 1994), 17.

292. Arnold Fruchtenbaum, *Footsteps of the Messiah: A Study of the Sequence of Prophetic Events* (Tustin, CA: Ariel Press, [1982] 2003), 99.

293. Fruchtenbaum, *Footsteps of the Messiah*, 102–03.

294. Fruchtenbaum, *Footsteps of the Messiah*, 102–03.

295. Randall Price, *Jerusalem in Prophecy: God's Final Stage for the Final Drama* (Eugene, OR: Harvest House, 1998), 219.

296. Fruchtenbaum, *Footsteps of the Messiah,* 105.

297. John F. Walvoord, *Prophecy in the New Millennium: A Fresh Look at Future Events* (Grand Rapids, MI: Kregel, 2001), 61–62.

298. Benjamin Netanyahu, *A Place Among The Nations: Israel and The World* (New York: Bantam Books, 1993), 23–25.

299. Fruchtenbaum, *Footsteps of the Messiah,* 311.

300. Cited by R. C. Sproul, *The Last Days According to Jesus: When Did Jesus Say He Would Return?* (Grand Rapids: Baker, 1998), 26.

301. John F. Walvoord, *Israel in Prophecy* (Grand Rapids: Zondervan Publishing House, 1962), 26.

## CHAPTER EIGHT

302. W. Graham Scroggie, *The Great Unveiling: An Analytical Study of Revelation* (Grand Rapids: Zondervan, 1979), 66.

303. Hanegraaff, *The Apocalypse Code,* 132.

304. Hanegraaff, *The Apocalypse Code,* 132.

305. Revelation 11:5 says, "And if anyone desires to harm them, fire proceeds out of their mouth and devours their enemies." Hanegraaff uses this to justify his metaphorical interpretation of the two witnesses. He says, "the two witnesses will not literally turn their mouths into blow torches on the streets of Jerusalem." (*The Apocalypse Code,* 133). The imagery of something proceeding out of someone's mouth is interpreted for us in Revelation 1:16 and 19:15, 21. These verses say that the resurrected, glorified Lord Jesus appears with a sharp two-edged sword coming out of His mouth. Of course, we know that Jesus doesn't have a literal sword coming out of His mouth. This is an obvious symbol for the Word of God that He speaks (see Hebrews 4:12). Yet, Hanegraaff would not say that because this symbol is used, Jesus is not a literal person. Likewise, he shouldn't say that just because this figurative imagery is used of the two witnesses that they aren't literal persons. The fire out of their mouths is symbolic of the fiery plagues they call forth on the earth during the tribulation. Again, the key to interpreting Revelation is often found within the book itself and consistency is very important.

306. Hippolytus, *Antichrist* 43. According to Bernard McGinn,

Hippolytus is also the first to state explicitly that the Antichrist will rebuild the temple in Jerusalem (*Commentary on Daniel* 4.49). Bernard McGinn, *Antichrist: Two Thousand Years of the Human Fascination with Evil* (San Francisco: Harper, 1994), 297n22.

307. LeRoy Edwin Froom, *The Prophetic Faith of Our Fathers*, vol. 1 (Wash. D.C.: Review and Herald, 1950).

308. McGinn, *Antichrist*, 67.

309. Froom, *The Prophetic Faith of Our Fathers*, 1:461.

310. McGinn, *Antichrist*, 67.

311. Hanegraaff, *The Apocalypse Code*, 133.

312. J. Dwight Pentecost, *Things to Come: A Study in Biblical Eschatology* (Grand Rapids: Zondervan, 1958), 308. Pentecost provides an excellent discussion of the various views concerning the two witnesses (304-308).

313. Hanegraaff, *The Apocalypse Code*, 237.

## CHAPTER NINE

314. Thomas, *Revelation 8–22, 279.*

315. Hanegraaff, *The Apocalypse Code*, 120-121.

316. Hanegraaff, *The Apocalypse Code*, 118.

317. Hanegraaff, *The Apocalypse Code*, 123.

318. Hanegraaff, *The Apocalypse Code*, 119.

319. Beale, *Revelation*, 849.

320. Hanegraaff, *The Apocalypse Code*, 235.

321. Hanegraaff, *The Apocalypse Code*, 122.

322. Hanegraaff, *The Apocalypse Code*, 121-123.

323. Charles H. Dyer, "The Identity of Babylon in Revelation 17–18," *Bibliotheca Sacra* 144 (October–December 1987): 441-43.

324. Hanegraaff, *The Apocalypse Code*, 1

325. Hanegraaff, *The Apocalypse Code*, 131.

326. Henry M. Morris, *The Revelation Record* (Wheaton, IL: Tyndale, 1983), 355.

# CHAPTER TEN

327. Hanegraaff, *The Apocalypse Code*, 72.

328. Hanegraaff, *The Apocalypse Code*, 90.

329. BDAG, 992–93.

330. Ibid., 993.

331. Ibid., 271.

332. Vern S. Poythress, *The Returning King: A Guide to the Book of Revelation* (Phillipsburg, NJ: P & R Publishing, 2000), 34.

333. Hanegraaff, *The Apocalypse Code*, 160. Thomas Ice notes this contradiction in the partial preterist view of *tachos* and *engus*. Thomas Ice, "Preterist 'Time Texts'" in Tim LaHaye & Thomas Ice, editors, *The End Times Controversy: The Second Coming Under Attack* (Eugene, OR: Harvest House Publishers, 2003), 105.

334. Hanegraaff, *The Apocalypse Code*, 160.

335. G. K. Beale, "Eschatology," in *Dictionary of the Later New Testament & Its Development*, ed. Ralph P. Martin and Peter H. Davids (Downers Grove, IL: InterVarsity Press, 1997), 331.

336. W. Hall Harris notes that the phrase "last hour" can refer to a period of time, since Jesus used it to refer to the entire period just prior to His crucifixion until His return to the Father (John 2:4; 7:30; 8:20; 12:23; 12:27; 13:1; 17:1). Harris refers this time to the final stage of history between the two advents of Christ. W. Hall Harris III, *1, 2, 3 John: Comfort and Counsel for a Church in Crisis* (Dallas: Biblical Studies Press, 2003), 104–105.

337. D. Edmond Hiebert, *The Epistles of John: An Expositional Commentary* (Greenville, SC: Bob Jones University Press, 1991), 107–8. Marshall supports this same idea. He says that John used the reference to the "last hour" to stress the imminency of the *parousia* and the urgency of being ready for the Lord's coming at any time. I. Howard Marshall, *The Epistles of John*, New International Commentary on the New Testament, ed. F. F. Bruce (Grand Rapids: William B. Eerdmans Publishing Company, 1978), 148–51.

338. Hughes, *Revelation*, 16.

339. William R. Newell, *The Book of the Revelation* (Chicago: Moody Press, 1935), 362.

340. Thomas, *Revelation 1–7*, 56.

341. J. A. Seiss, *The Apocalypse: Lectures on the Book of Revelation* (New York: Charles C. Cook Publishers, 1900; reprint, Grand Rapids: Zondervan Publishing House, 1966), 23; Hughes, *Revelation*, 237, 241.

342. Poythress, *Returning King*, 35.

343. Robert H. Mounce, *The Book of Revelation*, rev. ed., New International Commentary on the New Testament, ed. Gordon D. Fee (Grand Rapids: William B. Eerdmans Publishing Company, 1998), 41; cf. Grant R. Osborne, *Revelation*, Baker Exegetical Commentary on the New Testament, ed. Moisés Silva (Grand Rapids: Baker Academic, 2002), 55, 59; Hughes, *Revelation*, 241; Thomas, "Dating Revelation," 198.

344. Osborne, *Revelation*, 55.

345. Alan F. Johnson, "Revelation," 416-17 in *The Expositor's Bible Commentary*, ed. Frank E. Gaebelein, vol. 12 (Grand Rapids: Zondervan, 1981).

346. George Eldon Ladd, *A Commentary on the Revelation of St. John* (Grand Rapids: William B. Eerdmans Publishing Company, 1972), 22.

## CHAPTER ELEVEN

347. Gary DeMar and Francis X. Gumerlock, *The Early Church and the End of the World* (Powder Springs, GA: American Vision, 2006), 126.

348. Richard L. Mayhue, "Jesus: A Preterist or Futurist?" *The Master's Seminary Journal* 14 (Spring 2003): 13.

349. For a thorough defense of the AD 95 date of Revelation, see, Mark Hitchcock, "A Defense of the Domitianic Date of the Book of Revelation," Ph.D. diss., Dallas Theological Seminary (December 2005).

350. While Irenaeus is recognized as the key external witness for the late date of Revelation, Hegesippus (ca. AD 150) is actually the first witness in support of the mid-nineties date of Revelation. H. J. Lawlor, "Hegesippus and the Apocalypse," Journal of Theological Studies 8 (1907): 436-44. Francis Gumerlock, who co-authored a book with Gary DeMar, recognizes that Eusebius used Hegesippus as a source for the late date of Revelation (*The Early Church and the End of the World*, 132).

351. Irenaeus *Against Heresies* 5.30.3.

352. Hanegraaff, *The Apocalypse Code*, 153.

353. Hanegraaff, *The Apocalypse Code*, 153.

354. Johann Jakob Wettstein, *Novum Testamentum Graecum*, vol. 2 (Amsterdam: Dommeriana, 1752, reprint, Graz, Austria: Akademische Druk-U. Verlaganstalt, 1962), 746.

355. Hanegraaff, *The Apocalypse Code*, 153.

356. Irenaeus, *Against Heresies* 2.22.5-6. Here is the statement of Irenaeus where he interprets John 8:52-29. But besides this, those very Jews who disputed with the Lord Jesus Christ have most clearly indicated the same thing. For when the Lord said to them, 'Your father Abraham rejoiced to see My day; and he saw it, and was glad,' they answered Him, 'Thou art not yet fifty years old, and hast Thou seen Abraham?' Now, such language is fittingly applied to one who had already passed the age of forty, without having as yet reached his fiftieth year, yet is not far from this latter period. But to one who is only thirty years old it would unquestionably be said, 'Thou art not yet forty years old,' For those who wished to convict Him of falsehood would certainly not extend the number of His years far beyond the age which they saw He had attained; but they mentioned a period near His real age, whether they had truly ascertained this out of the entry in the public register, or simply made a conjecture from what they observed that He was above forty years old, and that He certainly was not one of only thirty years of age. For it is altogether unreasonable to suppose that they were mistaken by twenty years, when they wished to prove Him younger than the times of Abraham. For what they saw, that they also expressed; and He whom they beheld was not a mere phantasm, but an actual being of flesh and blood. He did not then want much of being fifty years old; and, in accordance with that fact, they said to Him, 'Thou art not yet fifty years old, and has Thou seen Abraham?' He did not therefore preach only for one year, nor did He suffer in the twelfth month of the year.

357. Hanegraaff quotes Irenaeus favorably as one who helps "shed light on New Testament historical accuracy." Hank Hanegraaff & Paul L. Maier, *The DaVinci Code: Fact or Fiction?* (Carol Stream, IL: Tyndale, 2004), 45. If Irenaeus is reliable enough to shed light on New Testament accuracy, why isn't he reliable enough to tell us when the book of Revelation was written? Hanegraaff uses Irenaeus when he helps his view and discounts him when he goes against his view. This is poor scholarship.

358. Hanegraaff, *The Apocalypse Code*, 153.

359. See endnote 145.

360. Clement of Alexandria, *Who Is the Rich Man That Shall Be Saved?* 42.

361. Origen *Commentary on Matthew* 16:6 [PG 13:1385–86].

362. Victorinus *Apocalypse* 10:11 [PL 5:333].

363. Victorinus *Apocalypse* 17:10.

364. Eusebius, *Ecclesiastical History* 3.20.8-9; 3.23.1-2.

365. Eusebius, *Chronicle* PG 68:551-52.

366. John D. Woodbridge, ed., *Great Leaders of the Christian Church* (Chicago: Moody Press, 1988), 77.

367. Jerome, *Against Jovinianus* 1:26.

368. Jerome *Lives of Illustrious Men* 9.6–7. In *Illustrious Men* 61, Jerome mentions a commentary by Hippolytus, which is no longer extant, that is one of the two oldest commentaries on Revelation. While there is no way of knowing if Hippolytus discussed the date of Revelation, if he did, one can assume he accepted the Domitianic date since Jerome fails to mention any other date.

369. This statement is made in both Hank Hanegraaff and Sigmund Brouwer, *The Last Sacrifice* (Wheaton, IL: Tyndale House Publishers, 2005), 343–44 and Hanegraaff, *The Apocalypse Code*, 157.

370. Hanegraaff, *The Apocalypse Code*, 157.

371. Norman L. Geisler, "Review of Hank Hanegraaff's *The Apocalypse Code*" http://www.ses.edu/NormGeisler/ReviewApocalypseCode.html.

372. Hanegraaff, *The Apocalypse Code*, 156.

373. Hanegraaff, *The Apocalypse Code*, 157.

374. R. H. Charles, *A Critical and Exegetical Commentary on the Revelation of St. John*, vol. 1, International Critical Commentary (Edinburgh: T. & T. Clark, 1920), xciv. Donald Guthrie supports Charles' argument. Donald Guthrie, *New Testament Introduction*, 4th ed. (Downers Grove, IL: InterVarsity, 1990), 954.

375. Colin J. Hemer, The Letters to the Seven Churches of Asia in Their Local Setting (Grand Rapids: Eerdmans, 2001), 193-95

376. Jean des Gagniers, *Laodicâee du Lycos: Le Nymphâee; Campagnes 1961–1963* (Quebec: Presses de l'Universitâe Laval, 1969), 4–11. The report notes that after the earthquake in AD 60 Laodicea did not ask for imperial financial assistance. However, it also notes that the government of the Flavians was particularly benevolent toward Laodicea. The Flavian emperors were Vespasian, Titus, and Domitian who reigned from

AD 69–96. The report does not say what form this Flavian benevolence took, but the Laodiceans rewarded the Flavian favor by dedicating the amphitheater to Vespasian and a door or gate in the amphitheater to his son Domitian. This evidence points to a rebuilding process in Laodicea that lingered into the reign of Domitian, the final Flavian emperor. This supports the AD 95 date of Revelation.

377. Suetonius, *Domitian* 7.2.

378. Colin Hemer provides an excellent discussion of the Domitianic vine edict in AD 92 and its relevance to the local setting of the church of Philadelphia (*Seven Churches*, 4, 158–59).

379. Guthrie, *Introduction*, 957, n. 1; Hemer, *Seven Churches*, 4, 158–59; Arthur S. Peake, *The Revelation of John* (London: Holborn Publishing House, 1919), 90–92.

380. Eusebius, *Ecclesiastical History* 3.18.4.

381. Grazia Salice, "Antipas" (ezinearticles.com. Antipas,-An-Unknown-Saint-Mentioned-In-The –Holy –Scriptures-Hagiography—And-Iconography). The tradition of Antipas' martyrdom in AD 92 by being roasted alive in bronze bull comes from a Byzantine hagiographer named Simeon Metaphastes (AD 900-984). Salice notes that some believe that Antipas was martyred in AD 68 under Nero, but even if this less attested date is accepted it's still too late for Hanegraaff's mid-sixties date for Revelation.

## AFTERWORD

382. Eisegesis means to bring in your own meaning to a text.

383. Hanegraaff, *The Apocalypse Code*, 124. (emphasis original)